Reviews for "It's What We Do Together That Counts"

"Earl Heard is a Louisiana treasure. His book is a recipe for success, whatever the task. Earl's life is proof that faith in God, love of family and never, ever giving up are the keys to a productive, happy life and career. He looks at roadblocks and sees stepping stones. He looks at adversity and sees good fortune. He looks at a problem in the same way as the great industrialist Henry Kaiser — just another 'opportunity in work clothes.' Earl's story is a must-read for every business school student and for anyone who has the entrepreneurial spirit! I am honored to call him a mentor and friend."

— Dan S. Borné, president of the Louisiana Chemical Association

"Earl has offered us a unique insight into his extraordinary success! His life reinforces the leadership principles of faith, love, perseverance and an extraordinarily positive approach to life. He is truly an inspiration to those who face life's many challenges."

— Bud Howard, vice president of global operations for Volvo Rents

"Earl Heard dared to believe in his vision, stand on God's word and make friends in the course of good business. *It's What We Do Together That Counts* is a great American success story!"

— John Lake, president and CEO of Rain for Rent

"For anyone who believes there is no light at the end of the tunnel, *It's What We Do Together That Counts* is a must-read. Earl provides a wonderful treasure of inspiration and information for anyone, in any walk of life."

— Dr. Shirley A. White, president of Success Images

"*It's What We Do Together That Counts* is for anyone with a dream who is willing to accept the labors required of entrepreneurship and reap the benefits of lessons learned to attain success. Earl Heard's determination and endurance, imbedded with his faith in God, his love of family and his expressed personal appreciation and recognition of friends, serve as a lesson in the realization that no man can stand alone."

— John Quincy Adams, director of industrial safety for
Enterprise Products Partners

"'Perseverance prevails,' author Earl Heard tells us in his inspiring and informative new book, *It's What We Do Together That Counts*. His own life is certainly a testament to the truth of those simple words, as he relates through honest, introspective and sometimes heartbreaking stories of his own rise to great entrepreneurial success after more than a decade of crushing setbacks.

This book is part personal memoir, part Christian inspirational message, part collection of practical lessons for entrepreneurs — and the author weaves all these elements together in a plainspoken, earnest manner that anyone in business can relate to. One of the great things Heard illustrates in this book is that early failures in business ventures often set the stage for later success; they are an inevitable learning process that nearly every entrepreneur must endure. But you need the right mindset in order to survive, to keep going — and to keep taking risks. 'You can give up, or you can give it your all,' the author states.

Other highlights are the author's succinct '100 Tips for Achieving Peace, Happiness and Success,' and thoughtful quotes from hundreds of successful entrepreneurs on the keys to success in business and in life. A key to Heard's own success that comes through loud and clear in the pages of this book is his genuine appreciation for all the people who have helped him along the way, in good times and particularly in bad. Now that he has accomplished many of the goals he began striving for over forty years ago, he has put his incredible story of hard work, resourcefulness and perseverance on paper for the next generation of entrepreneurs to benefit from."

— Brian Hill, co-author of *Inside Secrets to Venture Capital, Attracting Capital from Angels, The Making of a Bestseller*, and the novel *Over Time*, a "financial thriller" to be released in September 2005

IT'S WHAT WE DO TOGETHER THAT COUNTS

IT'S WHAT WE DO TOGETHER THAT COUNTS

THE BIC ALLIANCE STORY

A STORY ABOUT FAITH
OVER ADVERSITY,
PERSEVERANCE, AND
ENTREPRENEURSHIP

EARL HEARD

EDITED BY MIKE BOURGEOIS & BRADY PORCHE

BIC Publishing
P. O. Box 40166
Baton Rouge, LA 70835-0166
(800) 460-4242
www.bicalliance.com

It's What We Do Together That Counts, The BIC Alliance Story:
A story about faith over adversity, perseverance and entrepreneurship

First Printing

Printed in the United States of America

ISBN: 0-9768310-0-7

Printed by Moran Printing
Baton Rouge, La.
Cover design and layout by
Denise Poché & Heather Abboud

Quantity discounts available. Dealer inquiries welcome.

This book and the life about which it is written are dedicated to a loving and forgiving God, who has given me the strength to overcome adversity through faith, hard work and perseverance.

This book is also dedicated to my loving wife Bodi, to our family, to our BIC Alliance teammates and members, and to our loyal supporters and friends in business and industry.

I would like to give special thanks to Mike Bourgeois and Brady Porche for their hard work and dedication in helping to make my dream of publishing this book become a reality. I also want to thank Heather Abboud and Denise Poché, whose exceptional cover design and layout skills helped make this product better than I could have imagined.

Foreword

I first met Earl Heard in the 1970s after the story of his success was already well underway. Even though I entered his story as though in the middle of a movie, my first impression was that he was the kind of guy who wasn't going to give up on anything he set his mind to — no matter what.

As communications director for the Louisiana Department of Economic Development at the time (later public affairs director for the Louisiana Department of Transportation and Development), I met numerous people in the course of my work who, like Earl, were seeking to become entrepreneurs.

Unlike most of the others, however, Earl stuck out in my mind as a guy who was actually going to get it done. My respect and admiration for him in that regard continues to this day, as does our relationship. And so it has come to pass.

This is his story, and I am very glad to be able to play a small part in helping him present it to you.

It is said that if you want to be successful, you should find a successful person to emulate. The story of Earl's success is one that illustrates "what can happen when we put God first in our lives." It is a story about his unique interpretation of the American dream, and it is one that you can adapt in such a way as to help formulate your own successful interpretation of the American dream.

Furthermore, it outlines Earl's successful quest to "build something special out of nothing more than faith, hard work, perseverance and the belief that anything is possible."

To continue in his words, it is also about "believing and practicing the principle of treating others the way you'd like to be treated and realizing that it's what we do together that counts."

Since the majority of jobs in the United States are created by small business, the contribution of entrepreneurs like Earl Heard to the vibrancy of our economy cannot be overstated.

So, read, learn, enjoy and prosper.

— Mike Bourgeois —

"Pray as though everything depends on God, and work as though everything depends on you."
— Pastor Peter Barefoot, Christian Faith Church, Brisbane, Australia —

"I don't want a penny more or a penny less than God wants me to have."
— St. Teresa of Liseux, "The Little Flower" —

Contents

Introduction

It is my fervent hope that the information contained in this book will be a blessing to you and your loved ones.

In all honesty, no successful person can say that he or she attained his or her success alone. I am no exception.

In fact, I could not easily list on these pages all those who have contributed to my success to date — particularly our marketing partners and the readers of the *Business & Industry Connection (BIC)* and *The Leisure Connection (TLC)*; as well as the users of Ind-Viro Search (IVS), the BIC Alliance's merger, acquisition and executive recruiting firm; and those who use our leisure outfitters and event planning services.

In gratitude for that assistance, and in an effort to help you achieve greater success in your life, I present this information to you as more of a guide than a narrative. I encourage you to glean information from these pages that you can use daily for the betterment of both your personal life and your business life.

I firmly believe that when we place God, family and friendship at the top of our priorities, instead of seeking fame and fortune at any cost, we find greater peace, happiness and success in our lives.

It has been said that to strike it rich, you must develop a niche. The kind of richness with which God has blessed my family encompasses far more than mere monetary success. For the truth is that financial success isn't the most important aspect of our lives that we should be concerned about enriching or bettering.

It is my fervent hope that the information contained in this book will be a blessing to you and your loved ones. It is also my prayer that you will share some of the "nuggets" you read here with others seeking greater peace, happiness and success in their lives. After you've read my story, you'll find additional words of wisdom not only from me, but also from a host of successful executives and entrepreneurs in different industries whom we've had the privilege to meet and interview over the past two decades.

The entire Bible can be summarized in a few words from Jesus Christ: Make God first and do unto others as you would have them do unto you.

— Earl Heard —

"You cannot be the slave both of God and of money ... Set your hearts on His kingdom first and on His righteousness, and all these other things will be given to you as well."
— Matthew 6:24 & 33 —

Reader Beware!

---

*My wife Bodi and I know both the joy
and the agony of entrepreneurship.*

The life of an entrepreneur is not for the lazy or the weak in spirit. Furthermore, if you're married and want to stay that way, it is important that your spouse be as strongly committed to your entrepreneurial dreams as you are. My wife Bodi and I are blessed to have come from families with entrepreneurial backgrounds whose marriages had weathered the storms accompanying the rollercoaster ride of entrepreneurship. This didn't make our journey easier, but it at least helped us to know what lay ahead.

Bodi and I have not only known folks who have gone from rags to riches, but also those who have gone from happy, financially comfortable lives to poverty and overwhelming sadness in the quest for entrepreneurial success. Our lives have been shaped by our adversities and touched by people we've known who have experienced divorce, bankruptcy, family feuds, depression, addiction and even suicide as direct results of failing to achieve their entrepreneurial dreams. Yes, we know both the joy and the agony of entrepreneurship, but we are thankful that we can count ourselves among the minority of entrepreneurs who have lived up to their aspirations.

At one point in writing the BIC Alliance story, I came to a crossroads — I could have focused either on the positive things that have occurred during our lifetime or I could have launched into 100 pages of "woe-is-us" tales.

3

I could have written about all the hundreds of horror stories that Bodi and I, along with millions of other entrepreneurs, have lived. I could have gone into detail about letting down loved ones and friends, going without a vacation for 15 years and the stress of not knowing if you'll make it financially from one day to the next.

I could have described in great candor experiencing such things as the deaths of loved ones, merciless ridicule by peers, separation from family, divorce, bankruptcy and tax problems. I could tell you about the many folks who told Bodi and I we'd never rebuild our marriage or have a successful business. I could have told you about the day a banker told Bodi to get out of a drive-in lane because our car was smoking so badly or how the roof of an apartment in which we once lived fell in during a heavy rain. I could have talked at length about driving dilapidated cars and trucks that would break down on the way to work or about having to barter for food and lodging. I could have related one instance in which I flew to Dallas out of desperation in the middle of the night, using my dad's credit card for the fare, to try to sell a business that I'd poured my heart and soul into for pennies on the dollar — only to have my plea laughed at.

Some folks with whom I've spoken about this story have reminded me of an age-old journalism rule — if it doesn't bleed, it doesn't lead. Others have suggested that by sharing how excruciatingly difficult our lives were from 1980 to 1994 — the BIC Alliance's formative years — it might inspire folks either to hang in there when the going gets tough or to forget about becoming an entrepreneur at all.

However, my response to this has been the same all along. It's true that a lot of things have happened in our lives and to others we know that we'd never wish on another living soul — many of which we will touch upon in this story. But every form of adversity that

Bodi and I have faced has ultimately brought us closer to God and one another. We've since learned to focus on the positives of today and the opportunities and adventures of tomorrow rather than dwelling on the past.

We hope this story will help to inspire those who wish to become successful entrepreneurs and/or business executives to persevere and maintain close relationships with those who care about them along the way.

More than 30 years ago, Bodi and I got some advice from the proprietor of an RV dealership that we'll never forget. The dealer told us that in our travels there would be times when we would journey down a road for miles, only to learn that our destination is closed. Our only option would be to back out carefully and start over. His words of wisdom were, "Always remember that you started out to enjoy an adventure that you'll remember for a lifetime."

Your lifetime is an adventure to be enjoyed. We hope the road we've traveled along, with its various dead ends and detours, will inspire you and help to make your journey easier and happier both at work and at home, whether you're a successful entrepreneur or are just trying to make ends meet.

In my Alligator Management & Marketing seminars and keynote presentations, I utilize plenty of stories because people seem to remember stories and will relate personally by imagining themselves as the characters. Jesus, the greatest storyteller of all, often used stories in the Bible to help people learn and remember.

I figure that if this technique is worthy of the greatest teacher who ever lived, it's good enough for me.

Part I:

The BIC Alliance Story

A Childhood of Entrepreneurship

*The one thing that has
remained constant in my life is
my willingness to work hard.*

In order to get an idea of where we're going in our lives, I believe it is important to know where we've been. In my life, I've been up and down more times than a rollercoaster. I've enjoyed great successes, but as in the Old Testament story of Joseph, I know all about being thrown into a pit, so to speak. Fortunately, I also know how to dig my way out one handful of dirt at a time.

Early in life, I learned to think of failures and problems as challenges, and this attitude has helped me to face and overcome obstacles in one way or another over the years. Let's face it — everyone has problems. But most of us like a good challenge, an adventure. So, isn't it better to think of the adversities we face as opportunities and turn them into doorways to adventure?

In order to accomplish this, the one thing that has remained constant in my life is my willingness

Our family moved to Baton Rouge, La., from North Louisiana after World War II. This photo was taken at a 1954 family reunion.

9

to work hard. A hard work ethic was instilled in me at an early age by my parents, Leo and Margie Heard, and by my aunts and uncles. One of my favorite uncles, my mom's brother Bobby Crump, was my first mentor and one of the hardest working people I ever met.

My parents were raised on farms in North Louisiana with the understanding that if they didn't work, they didn't eat. From early childhood, my brother George, sister Ann and I always had chores to complete. We cut grass, trimmed hedges, washed dishes, cleaned toilets and made beds. We were taught early on that if we were fortunate enough to have something, along with it came the responsibility to keep whatever it was in tip-top condition.

We were also taught to save for a rainy day. Kids often dream of receiving the gift of their first bicycle — I'm the only person I know who had to save his allowance in order to buy his own. Because I was taught to save, however, I didn't pout. Besides, the words of praise I received from my folks for having earned and saved the money to buy the bike made me just as excited as receiving it. My wife Bodi has a wonderful way of thinking about the importance of saving. She always insists that it's not how much a person earns, it's how much they have on hand when they need it that counts.

My parents not only expected us to do household chores, but also to be entrepreneurial. My dad came from a large family, and many of his five brothers and two sisters were entrepreneurs at different times in their lives — some succeeded and others failed, but the ones who failed always tried again, which was inspiring to me. (One of Dad's brothers, my Uncle Roby, was a journalist for the *L.A. Times* and used to mesmerize us kids with stories of Hollywood stars he'd met and written about, such as Clark Gable, Marilyn Monroe, John Wayne and Howard Hughes.)

George and I collected soda bottles to cash in for refunds, and we sold cold drinks at high school sports events on Friday nights and at LSU football games on Saturday nights. As vendors, we learned quickly that by lugging the drinks to the top of the stadiums instead of hanging out by the lower seats, we were able to make more money. This taught us that by working harder, we could reap greater financial rewards. In my life I've encountered many folks who want to succeed in life as much as they can, but aren't willing to climb to the higher elevations where the greater opportunities lie. Others, however, climb the ladder of success the same way George and I used to make the journey to the high seats of LSU's Tiger Stadium — one step at a time.

On some occasions, we were encouraged to combine the skills honed while doing our household chores with entrepreneurship. While other kids used their parents' lawn mowers to make money by cutting grass, my dad financed a lawn mower for me with the under-standing that I would hire George and that we would pay him back by cutting yards throughout North Baton Rouge.

The competition was keen, but George and I were able to build a loyal clientele because we would do additional things, such as cut-ting hedges, trimming sidewalks and raking — the things we knew quite well how to do because we always did them at home. As a child, I was fortunate enough to be able to take advantage of anoth-er great opportunity — selling a booklet called *TV Times* door-to-door. I bought those TV schedules for a nickel a piece and sold them for a dime during the early days of television, when there was no such thing as *TV Guide*.

Since the supplier would not take any returns, I learned quickly to keep selling until I was out of inventory. Likewise, time manage-ment was important because if I didn't complete sales before the first day of the TV schedule, my customers wouldn't buy the publi-cation.

11

While selling *TV Times*, I learned additional lessons about the importance of saving money. You see, if I wanted to grow my territory, I needed to tap these savings in order to pay in advance because neither the vendor nor my folks believed in advancing me the money with which I could buy the next week's supply of booklets.

Another memorable experience I recall from the days when I sold *TV Times* was the exhilaration I felt when using some of the money I saved to do something special for someone else.

On one occasion, my parents were on a trip to St. Louis, and my maternal grandmother kept us kids while they were away. Desiring to do something nice for our folks while they were on this journey, I used my *TV Times* savings to send them flowers along with a note telling them how much we loved and missed them. (My grandmother helped me because I was only about 10 years old at the time.)

This is my first recollection of having saved money for the specific purpose of giving to someone else, and it taught me the joy that comes from making someone else number one. Today, in my Alligator Management & Marketing sales and management training seminars, I share a secret from Les Gelpin's book, *People Smart* — when you make others number one, they will respond in kind.

Sink or Swim:
Turning Adversity Into Opportunity At The Pool

Learning to put yourself in someone else's shoes is one of the most important keys to success.

Among my crowning achievements in elementary school was being selected as captain of a group known as the Patrol Boys. The Patrol Boys were a troupe of about 20 fifth and sixth graders who helped younger kids cross the street before and after school. Our job required us to arrive at school earlier than the other students, and our days were not done until all the younger kids were safely escorted across the intersection near the school. This was the first time that I was given responsibility for the actions of others, and the experience introduced me to the world of management at an early age.

I learned important lessons about life during my elementary, junior high and high school years.

Another great lesson I learned at an early age was the importance of training.

I was one of those youngsters who was slow in developing athletic skills. By the time I was 12, almost every kid I knew already knew how to swim. I, however, didn't. My dad's approach to the situation came from the old "sink or swim" school, and his method of teaching involved taking me to a public pool during peak attendance (or, sometimes to a local river during family outings) and

13

throwing me into the deep end. Thinking I was going to drown, I'd cry and scream like a baby. Try to imagine the embarrassment I felt in a pool filled with my classmates and their parents or in a river swimming with aunts, uncles and cousins!

Several times before I was 12, I nearly drowned and had to be rescued by lifeguards and family members. In spite of it all, however, there was nothing I wanted to do more during the first 15 years of my life than learn to swim. As fate would have it, a lifeguard at Howell Park in Baton Rouge named Freddie

Freddie Marks, center, a lifeguard at Howell Park in Baton Rouge, taught me how to swim and became the first of my many safety mentors. Also pictured are Anthony Magee, left, and Billy Weinbrenner.

Marks soon came into my life, took me under his patient leadership and helped me overcome my fear of the water.

He taught me the basics of breathing and kicking as I clung with a firm grip to the side of the pool, and told me that if I listened to and practiced what he showed me, not only would I become a great swimmer, but one day I might even become a lifeguard. Freddie and his fellow lifeguards at Howell Park were the first of my many safety mentors.

Freddie's patience and encouragement helped me overcome my fears, enabling me to learn to swim. Once I did learn, my new dream, which Freddie helped spark, was to become a lifeguard so that I too could help non-swimmers master the art. At 15, I got a job at the pool as a basket room attendant, which enabled me to practice swimming every day. By the time I was 16, I had earned my lifeguard badge and was a lifeguard and swimming instructor at the local pool. (Freddie, my mentor and friend, was lead lifeguard.) In the next two years, I taught children, adults and handicapped people to swim and saved numerous lives, considering my lifeguard job

14

to be the best in the world.

God blessed me with the ability to train others, and having progressed from near drowning victim to lifeguard taught me that anything is possible. I turned adversity into an adventure, and the experience ignited a fire in me for training and a love of adventure that still burns today.

Over the past four decades, I have trained hundreds, perhaps thousands, in fire and safety, technical skills, management, marketing, and sales. I have taught people how to save lives, manage other people, conduct sales presentations and seminars, and build successful, multi-million dollar organizations. I have also counseled many folks who were starting new businesses — some of whom had lost everything in previous business ventures and were starting over.

I, however, was a slow learner who had to work very hard to succeed. Perhaps this is one of the reasons why I have always identified with the trainee and tried to imagine myself in his or her situation in every instance — learning to put yourself in someone else's shoes is one of the most important keys to success I know of. Remember — there is a world of difference between sympathy and empathy. While we need both, empathy is critical to leadership.

In Baton Rouge, like many other cities and towns across America, a railroad track separated the more affluent area of town from the predominantly blue collar area. Our family lived in North Baton Rouge near the industrial plants where most of the hourly wage earning folks lived. Having grown up in that environment has enabled me to become a better manager and entrepreneur because through these experiences, I have learned to empathize with others.

I have found that two of the most effective elements of training are repetition and encouragement. I've also learned that both trainers and trainees must learn to have patience and to make learning exciting and fun. As my good friend Charles "Peanut" Hull used to say, you should learn something new every day — and never stop.

15

From Football Cheerleader to Boardroom Cheerleader

---

*The only person we should
laugh at is the one we see when
we look in the mirror.*

Between junior high school and my attendance at LSU and
Louisiana College — a Baptist institution of higher learning in
Pineville, La. — several things happened that helped forge the kind
of person I would later become.

In the midst of all our entrepreneurial endeavors, my siblings
and I were expected to keep up our grades, which we did. I was an
above average student in high school — until I began taking alge-
bra, biology and chemistry. I always loved reading, English, social
studies and history and thought that one day I would become a history and social studies teacher.

In books, I found adventure — they helped fuel my desire for
achievement and success. My favorite books usually weren't fic-
tional. I loved reading about real life heroes and about the ways in
which entrepreneurs were able to build something out of nothing.
Since I grew up in the 1940s, there was no television in our home
until I was in the sixth grade — so, reading became an integral part
of my life early on.

I liked books about history in particular, especially autobiogra-
phies about American heroes such as George Washington, Abraham
Lincoln, Benjamin Franklin, Andrew Jackson, etc. In addition,
Civil War stories, including those highlighting figures such as
Robert E. Lee, Stonewall Jackson and Ulysses S. Grant were (and

still are) among my favorites. Today, my library at home is filled with pictures of Civil War heroes and I often spend time studying photographs of both generals and soldiers.

On Saturday mornings, we'd get to go downtown to the movies, where we'd watch good cowboys like Roy Rogers, Gene Autry and the Lone Ranger in their white hats track down the bad guys in their black hats. Every great cowboy had a sidekick who was there through thick and thin — Roy Rogers had Dale Evans and Gabby Hayes, the Lone Ranger and Tonto, etc. This taught us kids that when push comes to shove, our success in life depends on doing right and having a good sidekick or two in our corner. Like all families, we occasionally squabbled among ourselves, but in times of adversity, we stuck together. These experiences taught me early on the role of teamwork and networking in success, whether it be in business or in one's personal life.

I cannot overestimate the role that my participation in extracurricular activities in junior high and high school — such as the Thespians and the Journalism Club — played in shaping my future. Upon joining the Journalism Club, I took the subject as an elective. Since I was poor in spelling and had no creative design skills, the teacher, Mr. Case, concluded that the only way I could pass the class was to coordinate sales for the school newspaper, another destiny-shaping development.

Mr. Case loaned us his car to make sales calls. It didn't take long before it dawned upon me that I could seize the opportunity afforded by access to this automobile to become an even better sales coordinator.

So, I came up with an idea involving the use of Mr. Case's car as a motivational tool for our sales team, and it worked very well. Teenagers all, whichever of our sales crew members sold the most each day got to drive the teacher's car back to school from the sales

17

calls. My lifelong friend Edwin Butler and I were the top sales producers. As you might imagine, I could hardly have chosen a more powerful motivator for this age group. As a result, sales took off, and we were very successful.

During the ninth grade at Prescott Junior High School in Baton Rouge, I considered going out for football — not because I liked playing football or was gifted in sports, but because football players were among the most popular kids in North Baton Rouge. Even more importantly than that, however, the girls seemed to be attracted to athletes and popularity.

In the late 1950s, Istrouma High School and arch rival Baton Rouge High School typically ranked among the state's championship teams in class triple-A sports. Football was king in Louisiana at that time, just as it is today. It was typical to have more than 20,000 people in attendance at an Istrouma High School football game on any given Friday night. On Thanksgivings when we were kids, our family would travel all the way to North Louisiana to attend the annual Haynesville High School-Homer High School football game, then onward to Shreveport to watch LSU play the University of Arkansas.

So, those involved in sports were the heroes of the day. By the time I was in junior high, I had stopped selling drinks at high school football games, but continued selling them at LSU games until my junior year of high school.

Of course, nearly everyone who played high school football in Louisiana then dreamed of attending LSU and becoming an All-American like our high school and college heroes, Billy Cannon of Istrouma High and Jim Taylor of Baton Rouge High. (Another one of my childhood football favorites was North Louisiana's John David Crow, who later played for Texas A&M.) A lot of the young men of that era who played football at Istrouma Junior High and

Prescott High School later played on LSU's first national championship team in 1958.

So, there I was, a skinny, not particularly athletic kid who had dreams of fame and fortune on the gridiron. I'll never forget standing under the goal post watching the coaches and football players at practice. Seeing the coaches holler at the players while they limped to the sidelines, I couldn't help but wonder if football really was for me.

As I stood there agonizing about my athletic future, I was distracted by the cheerleaders and pepsters who were also practicing along the sidelines. Watching all of those beautiful girls jumping, laughing, dancing and having the time of their lives was like finding an oasis in the middle of the desert.

At one point, my brother, sister and I were all cheerleaders at different schools (myself at Istrouma High School, George at Prescott Junior High, and Ann at Winbourne Avenue Elementary School).

Laughter is soothing to the soul, and people always seem to like having others around who can make them laugh. In the midst of such merriment, and right in the middle of those beautiful girls, were a few male cheerleaders also having the time of their lives.

Right then and there, I made a monumental decision that I have never regretted — I tried out for cheerleading in junior high school and went on to become a cheerleader at Istrouma High School during the heyday of high school athletics in Louisiana. My brother and sister followed my lead, and at one point, we were all cheerleaders at different schools.

I loved cheering for winners and helping to provide the moral support that drove our teams to greatness on the football field, the basketball court and the baseball diamond. Cheerleading opened the door to a joyous high school experience filled with adventure. I got to ride to the ball games in the pepster bus, made lots of great friends and, with my confidence built and my social skills refined, I went on to be chosen the "Wittiest Boy" in my senior high school class.

From the outset, I learned that the only person we should laugh at is the one we see when we look in the mirror. All others, we should laugh with. Also, if something isn't funny for all, it's not funny at all. In addition, I learned not to be afraid to march to the beat of a different drum and to focus on my own strengths. That's when I made the decision that I would go further in life by being friendly than I would by being smart.

So there I was, a popular cheerleader during the school year and a lifeguard at the most popular swimming pool in the summer — not a bad life for a skinny, slow learner with marginal athletic abilities. (As for my own athletic career, I did play church basketball as a youth, and the sport has become my favorite — to me, there is no better game for teaching teamwork and the art of the come-from-behind victory.)

I was even able to go on a few dates in my dad's 1950 automobile, which George and I kept spotless. I fondly remember Dad feeling the hood for warmth in the mornings after George and I came home from dates to see how late we'd stayed out. My folks always bought six-cylinder cars, usually with four doors, and never with whitewall tires. George and I each dreamed of days in which we could purchase vehicles of our own.

Little did I know at the time that one day my career would flourish as a cheerleader and trainer of fire and safety professionals, business and industry executives, and sales and marketing person- nel — and ultimately the owner of various luxury vehicles that I'd dreamed of owning since my youth.

Finding the True Love of My Life the Hard Way

I am living proof that
perseverance prevails.

The religious beliefs of my parents, who regularly attended church for Sunday services and Wednesday night prayer meetings, greatly impacted the first 20 years of my life. I accepted Christ at an early age and attended church regularly, but more in an effort to please my parents than to become a strong Christian. I do remember, however, becoming so inspired by the word of God on one occasion that I attempted to read the Bible from cover to cover. I didn't quite meet that objective, but I did find many wonderful stories that have meant a lot to me and have read it regularly throughout my life.

Because of my family's devotion to the Baptist faith, I attended a summer youth camp one year in Ridgecrest, N. C., where I met my first love and learned another monumental lesson about life in the process. She was a devout Baptist and an honor student at a high school in Shreveport, La. We planned to attend Louisiana College together when she graduated (I was one year ahead of her).

As time progressed, the fact that I didn't quite meet the expectations of her family — especially her older sister, who was a beauty queen and an honor student and dated a football star — wasn't as devout a Baptist as she was and hailed from South Louisiana eventually took a toll on our relationship. Since my family didn't have much money — my allowance was a meager $5 a week — I never owned a vehicle and had to hitchhike to Shreveport from Baton Rouge for visits.

Because my girlfriend's sister also attended Louisiana College, I could occasionally get a ride back to Pineville from Shreveport with the family. One Sunday after church, her parents drove her sister and me back to Louisiana College, and my girlfriend came along for the ride. Just north of Natchitoches, La., we encountered a young man hitchhiking. I noticed that he had a Northwestern Louisiana College insignia on his travel bag. Being a fellow college hitchhiker, I suggested that her dad give the young student a ride, and he did.

The young fellow was in the car for less than 20 minutes, but that was plenty enough time for him to become acquainted and mention that his half-sister attended the same high school as my girlfriend. This good deed that I innocently recommended on behalf of this young stranger set the stage for consequences I could hardly have imagined and definitely did not intend.

About six weeks after this fateful event, I went back to Shreveport only to learn that the hitchhiker was now dating my first love and that our courtship was finished! Broken hearted, I hit the road hitchhiking in the middle of the night, crying the whole trip.

During my days at Louisiana College, money was so tight that my friend and roommate Edwin Butler, right, and I had to hitchhike to get around.

As I walked along the highway that night with only the moon to light the way, I prayed to God to relieve my pain and to help me find

23

the true, lasting love of my life.

God answered my prayer less than two years later when I met my future wife — Mary Alice Bodi, or "Bodi," as she is commonly known. But as I continued along that dark highway on that heart-breaking night, I pondered over the reasons why the hitchhiker was chosen instead of me. (I surmised that it was due to the fact that his family had more money than mine, and, therefore, he seemed to have a more promising future.)

The pain of that night helped me to clearly realize that just because we think we're headed in the right direction doesn't necessarily mean that there isn't an alternative path God has planned that might bring us greater peace, joy and happiness. I resolved from that day forward to set my goals higher, work harder, earn more and win greater respect from those I cared about.

By the time I arrived in Pineville in the wee hours of the morning, I had convinced myself that a better, happier life lay ahead and all I needed to do was go for it. Looking back upon that incident of more than four decades ago, I'm certain God positioned the hitch-hiker on that highway for everyone's sake. Up to that point, my dream was to become a junior high or high school history teacher and basketball coach (both admirable careers) — instead, God directed me to become an entrepreneur and a trainer of men and women. Today, I am one of the happiest husbands, fathers and grandfathers I know, and I am enjoying the fruits of having built from scratch one of the most successful industrial marketing and communications businesses in the southern United States. What's more, Bodi has been a better wife than I could have imagined and an inspiration to me in good times and bad.

The point I'm making is that it's all about mindset. You can give up, or you can give it your all. I have always given it my all and have worked to help those who do the same.

24

Once you're in the pit of adversity, you are presented with only two choices — dig harder and climb out, or do nothing and get covered with dirt. I am living proof that perseverance prevails and that tomorrow will be better than today if you believe it will. When adversity rears its ugly head, just put on your inner smile and say to yourself, "Here I go on another adventure."

A Career Forged by Explosion and Fire at Ethyl Corp.

In times of crisis and opportunity, we need to think three dimensionally and take a few seconds to weigh our options.

In 1962, after having attended college for several years, I left and became a bricklayer apprentice and, later, a journeyman carpenter with Union Local 1098 in Baton Rouge. Looking back, I often wish that I'd finished college — these days I encourage everyone to get as much formal education as possible. I do believe, however, that the key to success in business involves more than just a college education. It requires a lifetime of learning, a willingness to work hard, and, most importantly, the ability to communicate and empathize with others.

My mother, God bless her soul, was my greatest role model. When I dropped out of college, she took me to my Uncle Bender and asked him to give me the hardest job he had in hopes that the experience would provide an incentive for me to return to school.

For several years, I worked on a number of commercial and industrial construction jobs in South Louisiana. During the weeks, I did carpentry work, and on the weekends, I mixed mortar and learned how to lay brick (mixing mortar with a hoe and keeping up with the bricks and scaffold for three bricklayers certainly helped to make a man out of me).

When I was in my early 20s, I spotted about 20,000 bricks stacked in front of a beautiful home while driving around. I stopped, knocked on the door and asked the owner if he and his wife had chosen anyone to lay the bricks, which were to be used to build fences, flower beds, etc. He told me they were in the process of getting bids and asked if I knew someone who could do a good job.

Even though I'd spent much more time chopping mortar than laying brick, I knew how to bid work and told the man that I'd like to bid for the job. I gave him a price, along with an estimated date of completion, and asked him if it was permissible to work on weekends. Surprisingly, he accepted, and I got the job, which I immediately subcontracted to my older friends. We attacked the project in earnest and we pushed hard for completion, since we each had day jobs.

As long as we were building fences and were being paid by the thousand, things went well. But when we got to the slow and tedious work, such as building flower beds, my older partners no longer wanted to see the project through, so they loaded up and headed home.

Since I'd made a promise to complete the job by an agreed upon time, I had no choice but to work throughout the night, using only the headlights of my car to light the area. Upon completion the man encouraged me by claiming that he'd selected me over more experienced craftsmen because he sincerely believed that I'd accomplish what I said I would. In the end, his words of praise meant more to me than the profits gained from the job. Another day, another valuable lesson about the importance of hard work — and keeping promises!

My fellow bricklayers were a lot of fun to work with, and they picked on me a lot. They taught me the importance of having fun at work through friendly competition and how competition can be used as a motivator for reaching a common goal. As laborers, we competed over who could mix the most mortar, and the bricklayers competed to see who could correctly lay the most brick in a day. On one occasion, I chopped mortar for an entire day and earned $20 in cash. That evening, I left in such a hurry to get home for a date with Bodi that I passed another car on the shoulder of the road and was ticketed by a police officer — the fine was $24. Despite my pleas, the officer cut me no slack. To this day, when I see someone in such a hurry that they take an unnecessary risk, whether it be on the road or in the game of life, I recall this experience. (Let us all remember the lesson outlined in the story of the tortoise and the hare — going about things in a slow, deliberate pace can often lead to greater success than taking the path of haste.)

Bodi and I were married on August 30, 1963. Not long after, she graduated from beauty school and became a hair stylist. We worked hard and saved our money, and six months after our wedding, purchased our first home. The down payment was produced by my

Bodi and I were married on August 30, 1963.

friends and family, who also helped us lay brick one weekend.

In 1965, we were in Monterrey, Mexico, on our first vacation enjoying the city's attractions when I returned to our hotel to retrieve some pocket money. That's when I received a call from my mom, who had tracked me down through the U.S. Consulate in Monterrey, informing me that I was to report for a job interview with Ethyl

Corp. (now Albemarle.) Bodi and I left for home immediately, driving almost 18 hours straight through without any sleep.

During the interview, I ran a 101-degree fever. The Ethyl executive interviewing me asked how badly I wanted to work for the company — when I informed him that I'd driven all the way from Mexico, he was quite impressed. Despite my discomfort, the interview went well, and I was offered the job. I went to work as an operator trainee at Ethyl thinking I had died and gone to heaven. No more would I have to worry about rain-outs and strikes, hindrances common to carpentry work and bricklaying.

Out of that experience, I learned the importance of being able to switch course quickly in times of adversity — or, better yet, of opportunity. (I also considered it a miracle that my mom was able to track us down in a city of nearly 1 million people.)

From my first day at Ethyl as an operator trainee, I was confident that the rank of supervisor was an attainable goal. Having come from the hard-work environment of bricklaying and carpentry work, I knew that no job at Ethyl would be more physically challenging, but I also knew that without a formal education, I'd have to work harder and perfect my people skills. On the other hand, I knew quite well how to compete fairly and to make work fun for myself and others.

Now, I thought, all I needed to do was learn the jobs and learn how to manage people.

At Ethyl, I learned about mentor-protégé relationships; effective people management skills; proper responses to life-and-death situations; and the importance of keeping personal journals and daily activity reports — the simple act of writing something and referencing it afterward is one of the best learning techniques in the world. I also learned about the importance of networking with industry peers and dealing effectively with change.

There were dozens of great mentors at Ethyl, but the ones who stand out the most in my mind included Joe Andre, a foreman who was also an entrepreneur in his spare time; Ted Crawford and Hodgie Fredericks, other foremen; Plant Manager Merlin Keonecke; Superintendents Quentin Hall and Dale Motsinger; and the other good men who became foremen or supervisors along with me — Charles "Peanut" Hull, Henry Currie, Jules Leblanc and George Newbill.

Fire fighting professionals from the Houston area were participants in the production of "Basic Fire Fighting Techniques" in 1981. They are: bottom row, Lee Ray Kaderli, W.E. "Buddy" Irby, Earl Heard, and Ray Patrick; top row, Raymond Harper, Gayle Vaughn, Jim Curl, Joe Eddleman, Donald Lawrence, and Robert A. Rakestraw.

During my tenure at Ethyl, I also met some of the best fire and safety trainers in the world, including the legendary Red Adair; Bill Koen of Exxon; Buddy Irby of Mobay; John Quincy Adams of Enterprise Products Partners; Carol Herring of the LSU Fire and Emergency Training Institute; Boots and Coots; and Dwight Williams and his dad, Les Williams, of Williams Fire and Safety (now Williams Fire and Hazard Control). Nicky Prejean of Southland Fire & Safety Equipment and Dave Dewey of Vallen (now Hagermeyer) also became good friends of mine and were early supporters of *BIC*.

Early on in my Ethyl career, I was assigned to operator Joe Andre, who was promoted to foreman shortly after. Mr. Andre advised me to get on shifts with older, more experienced operators who would take me under their wings and show me the ropes. He said this would provide a better learning experience than shifts of younger men who would spend a lot of their time talking about leisure activities and football.

Now don't get me wrong. I loved leisure activities and football as much as anyone, but I knew that the more money I earned, the wider my range of leisure options would be.

Mr. Andre also stressed the importance of listening closely, especially to instructors and even the sound of equipment. He and my other mentors at Ethyl taught me not only to listen, but to speak up by asking questions first. (In later years, I developed a process called "Listening for Success" for my Alligator Management & Marketing seminars that I learned and practiced in industry.)

Mr. Andre told co-worker Robert Wasson (now deceased) and me that, in our relationship, he would be the brains and we would be the brawn. He also said he would take credit when we did things right and blame us when things went wrong, and that he would share everything he knew with us, but if there was any hard physical labor involved, or a fire, an explosion, etc., we'd have to handle such situations.

He also shared with me how shift work could be used to our advantage and how by working on our days off, we could increase revenue, start a business, etc. In time, we grew to love and respect Mr. Andre, and he treated us like his sons.

Two months to the day after starting work, I experienced my first industrial explosion and fire when the Number Four Ethyl Chloride Plant blew up right before my eyes (I was loading a tank car about half a mile from the unit.)

Frank Richardson — one of my first supervisors and best friends and the first person to arrive at the tank car location — showed me how to isolate the lines to and from the Number Four Unit. I learned that you shouldn't try to extinguish a hydrocarbon fire completely, but must cut off the fuel source instead. You should also keep the unit cool and let the fire burn out in a controlled environment. (Extinguishing such a fire would leave a vapor cloud that could find a new heat source and create an even bigger explosion and fire.)

Almost 40 years ago, I learned through this and other experiences that in times of crisis and opportunity, we need to think three dimensionally and take a few seconds to weigh our options.

That day, I saw firsthand the importance of teamwork and training. I also learned how to interact with Exxon and other nearby plants and how mutual aid brought together the best firefighters in the area in only minutes.

We fought that fire, shut down nearby units and cooled the area without relief for more than eight hours. Even though estimates of damages totaled in the millions of dollars, we were thankful that no one was killed. After the fire, I was assigned to a maintenance turnaround group and worked 12 hours per day for several months until we got the unit back on line. I learned so much that day about the importance of fire and safety training that I spent the rest of my career at Ethyl as a member of the fire brigade and later became an instructor. Having seen friends and loved ones killed and severely injured on the job and off has made me a lifelong advocate of safety awareness in both settings.

During the next 15 years, I rose from operator trainee to operator, foreman, assistant general foreman, general foreman and ultimately to training coordinator for the entire hydrocarbon operations department. It took me from 1965 to 1970 to make foreman and, during that five-year period, I turned down overtime only twice. My co-workers nicknamed me "Cabbage Hog" because not only did I take all the overtime offered, but I also maintained my journeyman carpentry membership in Union Local 1098 and worked most of my days off and vacations on major construction jobs and/or turnarounds at local plants. (My mother-in-law, Yvonne Bodi, was the secretary for the Carpenters Local Union, and she always helped me get extra work when available.)

Since I was weak in chemistry and a slow learner, I knew I had to work harder and study more than most of the other operators at Ethyl. I also noted that companies will offer advancement opportunities to those who want to get ahead rather than those who just want to get by.

I learned early on that if you want to advance within an organization, you should keep company with those who share your mindset. So, while many of my cohorts shot the bull or cooked their favorite Cajun foods, I'd spend my free time tracing line or talking with the old timers about what to do during emergency conditions, fires, etc.

A volunteer for Ethyl's fire brigade, I also trained extensively with the fire schools at Texas A&M, LSU and Lamar, and offshore with Bill Koen. Video was just being introduced as a training tool, so I learned how to shoot, edit and produce training tapes. Even before the days of video, I produced Super 8 home safety tapes for my safety meetings at Ethyl.

My love for training enabled me to become a process trainer as an operator and later as a foreman. I became active in the American Petroleum Institute's (API) Training Conference, which brought together the best refinery and petrochemical trainers in the world to share information with one another. I also became an active member of the American Society for Training and Development (ASTD).

Ethyl was a wonderful place to work because the company was committed to training, providing opportunities to any employee interested in becoming involved in its training programs. The Gottwald family, who were Ethyl's primary shareholders at the time, were strong believers in effective management and safety training, which made the company a great place to develop leadership skills.

In the mid-1960s, the Vietnam conflict was in full swing, and many of my friends were being drafted. Initially, those of draft age who were married and some who worked in industry were draft exempt, but that was to change. By 1966, I knew it was only a matter of time before I would be drafted. So, I joined the U.S. Army Reserve and was assigned to the 4010th Unit, based in Baton Rouge.

I went to basic training in 1967 at Fort Knox, Ky., and spent six years on active reserve status, attending monthly meetings and summer camps at places like Fort Polk, La., and Fort Hood, Texas. In order to make the meetings without losing pay, I'd have to swap my days off at Ethyl with co-workers. This, coupled with the fact that days off were determined by seniority, meant I worked about seven years with few weekends off.

My time in the Army Reserve taught me a new respect for America's armed forces, especially the career soldiers and drill instructors. At one point, I even considered converting my reserve status and joining the Army full time.

While in the Army Reserve, I was able to utilize my carpentry experience and training expertise and helped train fellow reservists throughout my six-year stint. Watching the methodical way in which the Army trained recruits enabled me to integrate many of its techniques into my operator and fire safety training at Ethyl and later as a training and management consultant.

The year 1970 was a pivotal one for me in my career and in my personal life. On August 6, Bodi and I became the parents of a beautiful baby daughter, Dane. It was by far one of the greatest moments of our life together. Later that year, I was promoted to wage roll foreman, becoming one of the

Bodi and I became the parents of a beautiful baby daughter — Dane — on August 6, 1970.

youngest foremen ever to be promoted during that period at Ethyl's Baton Rouge facility.

The transition from wage earner to management brought with it a whole new set of challenges and adventures. Instead of continuing to be viewed as one of the guys by my co-workers, I was now looked upon as an outsider. The fact that most of my fellow supervisors were about 20 years my senior brought on even more challenges.

There were times in the beginning when Bodi and I would attend social events only to be shunned by those who previously had been close friends of ours and/or who believed in a strong division between labor and management — not to mention those who had been put off by my then-inadequate management skills. This prompted us to turn another adverse situation into a blessing, as our response was to buy a boat and a travel trailer so that we could enjoy leisure activities such as fishing and camping on our own.

Since my status in the reserve and my seniority at Ethyl meant I was off on weekdays only, and since our daughter was at an age that allowed us to travel, we were able to see and enjoy the entire Gulf South. This drew Bodi, Dane and me closer together than ever and helped forge the great love for quality leisure time and adventure that we continue to share to this day.

Whenever we had free time, we'd hook onto our boat and trailer and take off on a camping adventure. Even though these excursions took place about 30 years ago, they inspired me to conceive and later launch *The Leisure Connection* in 2002.

Meanwhile, because I had little or no management experience, I had to learn about managing people at work the hard way and made numerous mistakes in my new role. In the beginning, instead of treating folks the way they would like to have been treated, I made the mistake of treating others the way they treated me. I learned through the school of hard knocks that treating others with respect accomplishes much more than taking a dictatorial approach. Thankfully, pros like Mr. Keonecke, Mr. Hall, Herb Olson and others took me by the hand — and, sometimes, the throat — and taught me to manage others with empathy, compassion and understanding. Under their guidance, I learned how to listen more, communicate better and always remember that there are two sides to every story.

On one occasion, my supervisor, Mr. Hall, called me to his office and told me that if I couldn't become a better manager, he'd be forced to cut me back to operator. I was crushed because I felt that I was doing a better job and getting more done than other new supervisors. However, Mr. Hall explained that it wasn't just a matter of getting things done, but, equally important, getting things done diplomatically.

He told me to go home, think about it and let him know if I could meet his standards. I went home disappointed, hurt and ready to resign from the job and return to employment in the construction industry.

Quentin Hall, who was my supervisor at Ethyl Corp., helped me to become a better manager by teaching me how to lead with empathy and understanding.

I'll never forget Bodi's response. She said, "Earl, how is it that these men who knew so much when they selected you as a foreman over dozens of other candidates now know so little? Don't you respect them enough to follow their advice and leadership?"

She closed by saying that she would always love me, but would respect me more if I'd listen to and follow the advice of the people who genuinely cared about me. The next day, I returned to Mr. Hall and the other management folks, the union officials, the shift workers and the maintenance crew and apologized for my behavior. Within a few years, I progressed from one of the least popular supervisors to one of the most admired and respected. This was one of the greatest triumphs of my life, right up there with becoming a lifeguard.

When asked why people chose my shift, they responded that they always knew where they stood with me and that, in times of crisis, I was a great leader because I put the safety of the men on my shift first. I learned how to apply the "TEAM" approach and that, "Together, Everyone Accomplishes More."

"It's what we do together that counts," became my favorite phrase almost 35 years ago.

A Rude Awakening

Sometimes the only way to
move up is to move on.

Ethyl Corp. had been good to Bodi and me — my employment there enabled us to carve out a comfortable living, and I learned myriad lessons about professionalism, training, management, and safety, among other things. By 1980, however, my interest in a lifetime career at Ethyl had dwindled. Instead of being excited about going to work like I'd been for several years, I began to think about career opportunities and adventures beyond the gates of the plant.

An entrepreneur once told me that the gates around any business or industrial facility are built not only to keep intruders from trespassing, but also to keep workers from leaving. I believe, however, that we sometimes build gates around our minds that confine our imagination and limit our opportunities for advancement by lulling us into complacency.

Don't get me wrong — I've known thousands of folks who retired from long-term careers in business and industry who've enjoyed every moment and still enjoy their lives to the fullest. Working at Ethyl had helped build my confidence and a network of contacts across industry, and it also made me fearless when it came to failure. I'd risen from an operator trainer to a general foreman and training coordinator in a relatively short period of time. I'd learned how to manage people effectively, face life-and-death situations like fires and explosions without fear, and deal with unions and disgruntled employees and the tedium of doing the same things day in and day out.

However, the thought of doing the same thing for another 30 years — not to mention listening to co-workers talk about how tough things were and how many great opportunities there were beyond the gates — inspired me to shoot for more. Besides, by the late '70s, there was great regulatory pressure from the newly formed EPA on industrial corporations across America to clean up their act. In Baton Rouge, Ethyl's main products were tetraethyl lead, a gasoline additive, along with ethyl chloride, VCL and several other chlorinated hydrocarbons that were more closely regulated due to environmental concerns.

Not only had Ethyl helped build my confidence and management skills, it also gave me the opportunity to meet and network with successful entrepreneurs like Mr. Andre, Nicky Prejean and dozens of others who dared to leave the confines of industry for the adventures of entrepreneurship. I'd watched my own dad, who went blind at age 38, build a successful business after being laid off from a plant only two months before becoming eligible for disability retirement and I'd witnessed

Nicky Prejean, founder of Southland Fire & Safety Equipment, was one of the first people I met who left the security of industry to start a business.

my uncles — Bobby Crump and my dad's five brothers — and my father-in-law launch successful businesses after having honed their skills as craftsmen, sales professionals, retailers and/or body shop mechanics. I'd also known many entrepreneurs who had failed, only to start over with the same level of enthusiasm they'd shown in their first runs.

The common thread that binds all successful entrepreneurs is that they are not afraid of failure. Even more importantly, they consider their initial failures as stepping stones toward success. After all, even Thomas Edison failed thousands of times before achieving what was arguably his greatest success — inventing the light bulb.

During my time at Ethyl, not only had I built a network of fire and safety and training professionals throughout the petroleum industry, but I'd also turned my hobby of producing home movies and training tapes into a successful part-time business. In 1980, I resigned my position, bid farewell to Ethyl and launched Videoscan, an industrial video production and training company.

Boy, was I getting ready to learn some new and painful lessons! From the day I resigned from Ethyl, things went downhill. Believe me, going downhill at full throttle is an adventure. Getting up one step at a time, however, is an even greater one.

Just prior to my resignation, Mr. Keonecke, one of the greatest men I've ever known, visited with me one on one. He thanked me for my devotion to duty, wished me well and told me that if I ever decided to return to industry to give him a call. I left the meeting with tears in my eyes and prayed that one day I could be such a great leader and a fine gentleman.

The story of the Business and Industry Communications (BIC) Alliance actually began on that day.

Bodi and I had worked hard for 15 years, saved our money, built a nice home, had a beautiful daughter and were happily married. Within two years, however, we were on the verge of losing everything, including our marriage.

Try to imagine a soldier going into battle ill equipped and without any training or leadership to follow. That's how it was when I launched Videoscan.

I did have a little experience: I had gone to New York in the late '70s to attend some basic video training workshops and worked on a few amateur video training productions while at Ethyl. I invested our life savings, along with all of my 401K money, into video production equipment and took out loans for about $75,000 at 18-percent interest, the going rate at the time.

Since I had little or no sales or marketing experience, I decided to produce a video training program on sales and marketing as a learning tool. I approached Butch Baum (now deceased), the leading insurance salesperson in the world at the time, and offered to produce a story about his life at my own expense in exchange for the opportunity to learn how to sell from the master himself.

In 1980, I approached Butch Baum, who was the leading insurance salesperson in the world, and offered to produce a story on his life at my own expense in exchange for the opportunity to learn how to become a professional salesperson.

I spent a month with Butch and produced my first video. Working with him was a great learning experience, but a financial disaster. By the time I began producing revenue-generating training tapes, I was heavily in debt, and advances in new video technology were making my equipment outdated and obsolete.

Through my network of contacts in the API, I launched the first video basics workshop in the southern United States and began training people in the industry on how to produce their own videos. My intention was to teach the folks in industry how to script and tape their own videos, which would give Videoscan the opportunity to do the post-production work, such as sound, editing, music, etc. After all, post-production was time consuming and few trainers had the time to do it.

I also offered reduced rates for production in order to get the rights to the stock footage so that we could produce generic training tapes on topics such as safety orientation and firefighting basics and train-the-trainer clips.

Over the next two years, Videoscan produced about 40 training videos and won the business and industrial training award at the Mardi Gras Film Festival in 1981 for a piece about the work of a clerk of court. Our biggest client was Tenneco Oil Co. in Chalmette, La. — we produced 17 tapes for Larry Hess and L.A. "Tiger" Pereira, then Tenneco's fire and safety manager and operator training coordinator, respectively. Our greatest commercial success was a film called "Firefighting Basics," which we produced with the help of Buddy Irby and a group of professional industrial firefighters from the Houston area. We sold more than 50 copies of "Firefighting Basics" to industrial and municipal firefighting trainers across America. The fire training schools at Lamar University, LSU and Texas A&M all used the film as a part of their industrial and municipal fire training programs.

Among the most interesting of my experiences in the video production business was my collaboration with legendary pool hustler Minnesota Fats, who starred in a series of 10 safety films that I produced in 1982. This collaboration came about after I had helped one of Fats' friends, a man known as "The Mighty Glove," shoot a television commercial. I never received payment for my work, through no fault of The Glove's own. That story was relayed to Minnesota Fats, who approached me to find out how he could help resolve his friend's debt. The weeks spent with the very colorful Fats were among the most interesting of my life. Paul Carroll, founder of Cherokee Scaffold and a pool enthusiast, helped pay the production cost, as I was on the verge of closing. We made it through production, but never had the money to edit the tapes, which we still have today.

In the beginning, I tried advertising my services in trade publications, but quickly discovered that among the big industry publications, none offered multi-industry content that reached across a wide range of sectors and job titles. For example, there were great publications for drilling and production, marine, pipelines, refining, hydrocarbon processing and petrochemical. The same was true for construction, pulp and paper, and power generation. This was great for publishers, but terrible for service companies.

In order to reach across all the markets, a service company that offered multi-industry products and services — such as equipment, training, fire and safety, environmental maintenance or construction services — needed to be in more than a dozen publications. There were some great vertical publications, but none were horizontal, crossing a wide range of industries and departments within them.

To make matters worse, the publications wanted merely to sell advertising space and would do little more than laugh at my request for editorial coverage of my company's history or access to their databases of readers for leads of potential customers. The only people who ever called me as a result of my advertising were people who wanted to sell me more advertising.

Once again, as I had done so many times before, I saw the possibility of turning a form of adversity into opportunity. The adversity that had been created by the people at those publications opened the door to a publishing adventure for me.

Out of frustration and with my capital dwindling, I decided to produce a training newsletter and mail it to train-

My first newsletter, News and Views from Videoscan, appeared in December 1980. The results were amazing.

43

ers across business and industry in the Gulf South. My first newsletter, *News and Views from Videoscan*, appeared in December 1980, and the results were amazing. Not only did we receive inquiries about our production and training services, but, more importantly, other industrial suppliers called to see if they too could utilize my newsletter to communicate their stories to industrial buyers.

I launched America's first industrial training magazine, The Training Coordinator, in 1981.

Like me, they needed a vehicle with which they could share their success stories and wanted to utilize a publication's database of readers for prospecting. The concept of a multi-industry, multi-departmental newsletter was so unique and promising that I decided to launch America's first industrial training magazine, *The Training Coordinator*, in 1981 instead of printing another newsletter.

Our feature story was about Tenneco and the training videos we were producing for them. The folks at Tenneco were truly visionary at the time and saw this editorial as an opportunity to promote their safety, environmental and community service activities. In those days, the phenomenon of an industrial buyer actually going on record talking about the products and services of a supplier was almost unheard of.

Little did we realize at the time that this was the beginning of a communications alliance between buyers and suppliers in industry — something that really didn't exist in this type of multi-industry format prior to 1981.

By the time *The Training Coordinator* was launched, it was too late to salvage Videoscan as a viable television production and training company, despite an excellent product. To make matters worse, the economy was terrible and many of the folks in industry didn't have the budget to buy or produce video training tapes.

Furthermore, instead of buying tapes, some people would rent and copy them, in violation of copyright laws. I couldn't help but be saddened that some of the very people responsible for helping train our future leaders saw nothing wrong with this practice.

During this time, I was working night and day on both ventures, and my family relationship suffered. My relationship with God also declined, and we seldom, if ever, went to church.

In 1981, my loving and supportive wife was pushed to the limit after I took out a second mortgage on our home over her objections. She suggested that, had I complied with her wishes, we could have saved ourselves years of suffering and hardship. She then recommended that I shut down Videoscan and throw all my time and energy into building *The Training Coordinator*.

Her logic was simple — the multi-industry publication was a winner, and Videoscan was a financial loser. Why not invest my efforts into something that industry wanted and supported? Instead of hoping people wouldn't copy our tapes, we'd encourage them to use our material to help educate and train others through pass-along readership.

Call it ego, shortsightedness or just plain stupidity, but I didn't heed Bodi's advice. As the Kenny Rogers lyric goes, "You've got to know when to hold 'em/Know when to fold 'em." I didn't "know when to fold 'em," and lost everything.

She co-signed a loan out of love, but told me that if I lost our home and couldn't put our family first, then I had the wrong outlook on our marriage and was putting it at risk. Like a fool, I tried to keep both the video production company and the publication active and ended up having to close both. At the time, I didn't know anything about product life cycles, market research or strategic planning, and it cost me dearly. I vowed to myself that in my next entrepreneurial venture, I'd not only learn how to sell, but to master the techniques of marketing as well.

By mid-1982, my family's faith in me was at an all-time low, and my relationship with God was limited to praying for survival.

Finally, I heeded Bodi's advice, laid off the production crew and tried to keep the publication going while I looked for a job, although by 1982, I was forced to shut down *The Training Coordinator* as well.

Always a believer in the power of networking, I went back to my friends Butch Baum, my longtime friend and Videoscan partner Bobby Davis, Mr. Keonecke and others. Butch told me that if wanted to start over in business that I should stay focused on the Gulf Coast and decline a job offer that I had received in the fall of 1982 from an oil company in Tulsa, Okla.

He also told me that if I really wanted to rebuild a happy marriage and, eventually, a successful business, I should remain close to my family. In addition, he informed me that most entrepreneurs fail on their first attempts at business ownership and that if I ever started another business, people who might have ignored me in my first endeavor would help me the second time around because, like many of them, I had the guts to start over. Time would prove him right.

Even though things had gotten rough, I remained confident in my decisions. You see, I've always been a strong believer in what I call "refraining from complaining," especially if the complainer isn't willing to make changes. For instance, when we see co-workers being promoted, instead of complaining about it, we should strive for promotions ourselves, especially if we sincerely think we can do better.

The same is true for entrepreneurship. Instead of complaining about how successful others are, why not prove you can do it yourself? My mom used to have a saying that there is no use crying over spilled milk. In addition, I never once heard my dad complain about getting laid off without benefits. His revenge was simply to live well and be happy.

When the time came that I felt I could do better for myself and my family, the fearlessness I'd learned at Ethyl was what had sparked my decision to move on. Even years later, after I'd lost everything and was working 12 to 14 hours a day, six or seven days a week, I never once regretted resigning from Ethyl to pursue my dream. If success has taught me anything, it's that if you're not satisfied, you should spend your time trying to make the situation better, and if that's impossible where you are, you shouldn't be afraid to move on. After all, sometimes the only way to move up is to move on. Like many entrepreneurs say, "No guts, no glory."

Climbing Back Up at Hill

Networking is one of the most important things a person can do in order to succeed in business.

Bobby Davis loaned me the money to pay my car note and survive until I found a job. I later learned about a training position at the Hill Petroleum refinery in Krotz Springs, La., from a fellow ASTD member and called my former boss and mentor, Mr. Keonecke, for a referral.

Mr. Keonecke called Hill Petroleum Plant Manager John Bender, who was gracious enough to interview me at 7 p.m. on a Friday night. Before returning home from the interview, I went to my office, which was shut down and devoid of furniture. I sat on the floor, cried and asked God's forgiveness for ignoring Him and my family and prayed for the job at Hill Petroleum.

I had reached bottom that night. I was in the pits again, lower than a snake's belly in a wagon rut, and the only way to go was up.

I loved God and my family too much to kill myself, so I decided that if I was going to die, I'd die working. It was then that I vowed to work night and day until I'd restored my relationship with God, family and friends.

The following Monday, I was interviewed again in Houston and hired by Hill Petroleum, in spite of the fact that many of the more than 700 other applicants held master's degrees and Ph.Ds. Even though I had never worked in a refinery, my training references and contacts with fellow refinery trainers convinced the folks at Hill that I was worth the investment.

Folks, networking is one of the most important things a person can do in order to succeed in business. The networking I did with my ASTD friend and Mr. Keonecke led to the interview, and it was then that I became a lifelong advocate of the practice. Although it doesn't always get you a job, it certainly can help you get in front of a decision maker. Networking not only helped me get the interview at Hill, it played a primary role in the phenomenal success of the BIC Alliance in later years.

Thus began my long road back. I was 40 years old and starting over in both my business life and my personal life. In the first week of July 1982, my mother had to drive me to Hill Petroleum because my vehicle wasn't dependable enough to make the one and one quarter-hour trip. Shortly thereafter, I purchased a trailer at False River in New Roads, La., with the help of a loan from my mom and dad (part of my employment contract with Hill stipulated that I live close to the plant).

After my first business failed in 1982, my parents helped me purchase this trailer on False River in New Roads, La., while I worked at the nearby Hill Petroleum refinery.

We survived on $500 per month for about a year in order for me to continue to pay the large note on our home in Baton Rouge, which we were trying to sell because of the high expenses incurred as a result of my business failure. We were so broke that our entertainment was limited to playing checkers and cards, fishing and enjoying cookouts. Dane and I saved our change to buy a Monopoly board game and joked about our "monopoly" fortune when we finally bought it.

During my year at Hill, I worked long hours. I began to use my spare time to engage in planning for my re-entry into industrial publishing. I read every book about sales, marketing and entrepreneurship I could get my hands on and began compiling a database of "who's who" in industry across America in order to build a list of prospective recipients of an industrial publication.

My refinery training friends, including Don Traigue and Otis Crawford of Shell and Tiger Pereira of Tenneco, helped me to develop a refinery training program at Hill, and many of my associates in API gave me input to help make our program a winner. In this way, I benefited from the fact that there is a brotherhood among people in business and industry built on mutual respect and a desire to help one another, especially in times of trouble and of opportunity.

By June 1, 1983, my mission at Hill, which was to train personnel for a cat cracker startup, was complete.

Even though my first business had been a bust, I was ready to climb out of the poverty pit and start over — it was more clear to me than ever before that failure was not an option. So, with only $3,000 to my name, I resigned from Hill, developed a prototype of the first cover of the *Business and Industry Coordinator (BIC)*, stapled it over a copy of *The Training Coordinator* and went back into business. I worked "half days" for the next 15 years (any 12 hours I chose, six or seven days a week).

A New Beginning

My experience in life-and-death situations at Ethyl, combined with the dire financial situation I was in during the early '80s, triggered an idea that would forever change the destiny of BIC.

It took from June 1983 to April 1984 to publish the first *BIC*. During that time, I also sold advertising for *Travelhost* magazine, conducted management and operator training for Placid Oil Co. and Tammco in New Iberia, La., and worked as a marketing consultant for the University of Southwestern Louisiana (USL) in Lafayette (now the University of Louisiana-Lafayette).

I sold the trailer, paid off my folks and traded advertising for a couple of rooms at the Bellemont Hotel in Baton Rouge in which to live and work. Bellemont owner A.C. Lewis had just

The first issue of the Business and Industry Coordinator (BIC) was published in April 1984. We were off to the races, even though it would take almost another decade to reach the pot of gold at the end of the rainbow.

built the Great Hall, a spectacular convention and meeting facility at the hotel, and hired Kent Wasmuth as sales manager. In exchange for living and office space and occasional access to food during happy hour, my job was to help Kent market the Bellemont and the Great Hall to business and industry across the

Gulf Coast.

From our humble beginnings on the banks of False River and the two rooms at the Bellemont Hotel, the BIC Alliance was launched. From the start, those offering hospitality, lodging, meeting and convention space became some of our first and most loyal clients. (My successful experience in the hospitality industry with these folks 20 years ago helped prepare the way for the launching of *TLC* in 2002.)

Many of these people, including Kent, who went on to become director of sales and marketing for Opryland Hotel and Conference Center in Nashville and later the Wyndham New Orleans Hotel at Canal Place, have been longtime supporters of both *BIC* and *TLC*.

My original vision was for *BIC* to be a business-to-business publication across South Louisiana and a business-to-industry publication across the Gulf Coast from Mobile, Ala., to Corpus Christi, Texas. This way, I could barter for essentials like food, lodging, office space and supplies and use the revenue from the cash sales to industry to cover products and services, payroll, printing and mailing.

Many times during the early years, I had money for printing, but no money for mailing. On several occasions, Bodi used the tip money she made as a hair stylist (or we borrowed from friends and family) so that we could afford mailings — even though I had broken her heart and lost everything it had taken us 20 years to build. If that wasn't enough, I had yet another financial disaster on my hands.

BIC was getting off to a great start, but *The Woman's Coordinator*, another publication I had started, was slowing the growth of the former and losing money. I was working night and day as publisher, salesperson and managing editor and was handling all the other duties of the business as well.

One evening, I made a cold call to Baton Rouge businessman Guy Bellello, owner of several health clubs, in order to talk to him about *The Woman's Coordinator.* As I proceeded to Mr. Bellello's office in the pouring rain, I wondered where in the world I would get the money to publish the next issue of either publication.

I was soaking wet when Mr. Bellello answered the door. Once we were inside, he offered me a beverage and began telling me about the upcoming 25th anniversary of his health clubs.

All of a sudden, he reached into his pocket and pulled out a money clip filled with $100 bills. It was the largest wad of money I'd ever seen, but I was even more flabbergasted at what happened next. Mr. Bellello threw the

My experiences with The Woman's Coordinator taught me the importance of conducting market research. As it turned out, most business women preferred to be featured in publications that appealed to both sexes.

money clip onto the desk in front of me and said, "Earl, I'm tired of seeing some of those women on the front cover of *The Woman's Coordinator* who aren't true entrepreneurs."

He went on to say that he wished to sponsor the next front cover of *The Woman's Coordinator* and feature his wife, Ginger, whom he considered a true female entrepreneur, and their business's milestone of 25 years.

Talk about turning adversity into opportunity!

My experience in life-and-death situations at Ethyl, combined with the gravity of the dire financial situation I was in at the time, somehow coalesced to trigger an idea deep inside my brain that would forever change the destiny of *BIC* and our family in one fell swoop. A light went on that would illuminate and pave the way for a successful future.

You see, even though I had been offering ongoing editorial and direct mailing as part of a marketing campaign in *BIC*, it had never occurred to me to offer a business the opportunity to invest in a front cover sponsorship.

As Mr. Bellello spoke, my mind raced at a rate of a thousand miles per minute. If he was interested in sponsoring a front cover of *The Woman's Coordinator* in order to recognize a person and an event, I wondered what someone else might be willing to invest to sponsor a front cover of *BIC* in order to promote a multi-million dollar construction project, a new product, etc.

As I unfolded the money clip and began to count the $100 bills, Mr. Bellello told me it amounted to $5,000. This unbelievable experience on a cold, rainy night after most people had quit for the day marked a spectacular turning point in my life. In less than 30 minutes, I had envisioned, with the prompting of Mr. Bellello's request, a way not only to keep *BIC* alive, but also to build it into a viable business venture.

As I drove off with the $5,000 contract in hand, I began thinking of more scenarios in which people would sponsor *BIC* covers in order to build market share; enhance public relations; gain exposure for successful projects and for events such as trade shows; announce mergers and acquisitions, etc. (Today, our front and back cover campaigns are our most popular and are usually reserved six months to a year ahead of key industry trade shows, conferences, events, projects, etc.)

The list went on and on in my mind to the point that I was barely able to sleep that night, experiencing the excitement of a child at Christmas and waiting impatiently for daybreak so I could begin offering sponsorships for *BIC* covers. (In my Alligator Management & Marketing seminars and during keynote presentations since that fortuitous day, I have continued to share with others the ways in which our minds can work during times of crisis and opportunity.)

Early the next morning, I began to contact industrial service company managers and entrepreneurs in order to sell them on this novel idea. One of the first people I contacted was Brooks Bradford, who owned an industrial service company called Mobile Air at the time. Mr. Bradford was not only a visionary entrepreneur, he also completely understood the role of marketing and promotion in the world of industry.

Almost on the spot, he agreed to sponsor the next cover of *BIC* for $7,500 in addition to three full pages on the inside for a total of approximately $12,000. Bingo — we were off to the races, even though it would take almost another decade before we would reach the pot of gold at the end of the rainbow.

With this new concept to help our marketing partners, I put Mrs. Bellello on the next cover of *The Woman's Coordinator* and Mr. Bradford and his company on the next cover of *BIC*. Shortly after that, I shut down the women's publication in order to focus more energy on *BIC*, which I expanded from four to six issues per year.

The demise of *The Woman's Coordinator* taught me the importance of conducting market research — as it turned out, most business women preferred to be featured in publications that appealed to members of both sexes rather than those focusing merely on women.

Sonny Anderson, founder of Anco and Basic Industries and a longtime BIC Alliance member, had kept *BIC* alive by co-signing a note several months earlier. As part of my agree-

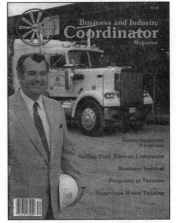

Sonny Anderson, founder of Anco and Basic Industries, co-signed a note to help keep BIC alive in the early '80s.

ment to ensure the success of his investment, he wanted me to tell him how I planned to make *BIC* a success. Not only did I promise to work from daylight until dark, but I also informed him that I was changing the publication's paper from "glossy" to newsprint, which was more economical and would enable me to put more into expanding readership.

When I converted from glossy to newsprint I searched for a printer that specialized in the latter and who would take a chance on a startup operation. Ralph Hay and his wife Josie of Dixie Web in New Orleans agreed to print our publication as long as we paid in full when each job was completed. That meant that we needed the money for printing and direct mailing at the same time. In those days, I'd stay awake all night watching press runs and waiting to get copies of the latest issue, which I'd deliver to our marketing partners in the morning. Upon delivery, I'd collect their payments and head to the bank to make a deposit so that I could get cashiers' checks from the post office to pay the printing bill. Thankfully, things have gotten simpler over the years!

Mr. Bradford appeared on the cover of our last fully glossy publication. (It would be 12 years before I'd return to a glossy format, and then only for covers.) The next issue of BIC was sponsored by Mack McDonald of Modern Valve, and a new concept in industrial marketing and communications was off and running.

A Baptism By Fire

*Our business would never have made
it had we not turned our early
challenges into great adventures.*

God works in strange and miraculous ways — my mom's death in 1986 was a perfect example of this. Mom's passing not only brought my dad and me closer together, it also helped me to realize how much Bodi and Dane loved me. Watching Bodi and Dane share my suffering was a wake-up call for me to focus first and foremost on rebuilding my own family and my relationship with God. On Valentine's Day 1987, Bodi and I renewed our wedding vows and from that day forward, both our marriage and our spiritual life has grown stronger each year.

That Valentine's Day was a turning point in our lives because Bodi and I vowed to one another to discuss only the positive aspects of our lives up to that point. We agreed that the past was the past and that the best way to have a

Valentine's Day 1987 marked a new beginning for Bodi and I. Shown here with Dane, we vowed to put the past behind us and only focus on the positive aspects of our life together.

wonderful future would be to focus on the positive. It is this promise that has factored in my decision to omit from this narrative some of our most heartbreaking experiences.

I recommend this practice to anyone who has faced trials with others, whether it be with a spouse, a family member, a friend or someone at work. It's been said that the greatest peacemaking words in the world are, "I'm sorry, it won't happen again." An integral part of preventing something negative from recurring is simply not discussing it or, even more importantly, not thinking about it.

In the early years, much the same as today, there were literally thousands of folks who helped keep *BIC* alive. First and foremost were our readers, who supported our concept, shared their expertise in articles and used the products and services of our marketing partners. Each advertiser who reserved space with us in the first few years took a chance that their ad and editorial might never appear in print because we were so under-capitalized.

In addition to our readers and advertisers, who often paid in advance in order to allow us to meet payroll and publishing costs, there were countless others who loaned me money and/or co-signed loans on pure faith. People like Sonny Anderson, Bill Brackman, "Big" Ernie Hernandez, Haskell Douglas, Ed Sakakeeny, Bobby Davis, Maxie Thiel and many others helped along the way. My uncle, Thomas Heard, and my sister and brother-in-law, Ann and Shahram Nickroo, all pitched in, and my brother, who had been a maintenance executive for Exxon, introduced me to dozens of industry contacts, many of whom later became BIC Alliance members.

But the two people who sacrificed the most were my wife and daughter.

For several years we lived on Bodi's income from styling hair so that every nickel generated from *BIC* could help cover expenses.

Dane worked during high school to help us make ends meet and paid for almost all of her college expenses. She, along with Bobby Davis, drove all over the Gulf Coast distributing publications. What we lacked in money, we made up for in hard work, perseverance and good humor.

After my dad lost his sight at age 38, he had no choice but to seek employment at a hospital concession stand for the blind, where he worked for more than 20 years.

After my dad lost his sight, he had no choice but to find employment at a hospital concession stand for the blind, where he worked from dawn until dusk six or seven days a week for

Without the support of my in-laws, Yvonne, left, and John Bodi, we would never have been able to persevere and, ultimately, succeed. Mr. Bodi, who owned and operated one of South Louisiana's largest body shops, was a great role model for me.

more than 20 years. As I've said before, never once did I ever hear him lament about the hand he was dealt. Without his inspiration and my mom's support, along with that of Bodi's parents — John and Yvonne Bodi — we would never have been able to persevere.

As an entrepreneur, my father-in-law was a great role model for me. Although he dropped out of school in the seventh grade, he went on to learn the automotive body shop business and became the owner of one of South Louisiana's largest independent body shops. Early on, he encouraged me to one day launch my own business. He also taught me the power of networking, hosting hospitality functions and sponsoring golf tournaments and other events, etc.

I still thank God every day for the blessings we received during that time and for the support we enjoyed, all of which encouraged me to work diligently toward a successful future for the BIC Alliance.

In those days, every bit of revenue we generated was used to pay debt and bankroll growth in order to reach a wide range of industries nationally instead of regionally. Bodi and I went without a week of vacation for almost 15 years and were once more than $600,000 in debt. We promised ourselves that we would always live on the bare essentials until we were debt free, a status we indeed achieved more than 10 years after the launching of *BIC*, thereby proving to all who supported us that they had not done so in vain.

Sadly, my mom, who had stuck by me through thick and thin, never got to see us turn the corner. Often times I look up into the heavens and imagine her as an angel smiling down upon our family and putting in a good word for all of us with God himself.

During the late 1980s, I spent more than 70 days a year on the road, mostly between Baton Rouge and Houston. Once, Mike Conners — a longtime friend of mine who worked with me at the time — and I drove to Pittsburgh for a trade show and took turns sleeping because money was so tight that we couldn't afford to stay overnight until we reached our destination. For several years Dad loaned me his credit cards when I traveled because my credit was too poor for me to get a card of my own.

To maximize time, I would come home on Monday or Tuesday evenings at around 6 p.m., eat supper, go to bed, get up at 9 p.m. and leave for Texas. I would arrive in Houston at about 2 a.m., sleep until 7 a.m., and begin my sales calls at 8 a.m. I would work until 6 or 7 p.m., have supper with a client or prospect, get back to my room around 10 p.m. and work until midnight on editorial content and/or my mailing list. On Thursday evenings, I would make the drive back to Baton Rouge in order to be able to put in a full day on Friday.

One weekend, Dane came home from Chamberlain-Hunt Academy in Port Gibson, Miss., where she was attending high school. She and I, along with Bodi, sat on the bed in an apartment one evening and had a long and emotional discussion about our future. As we cried together, they asked me to consider shutting down *BIC* and going to work in industrial sales. I explained, however, that even if I made $100,000 to $125,000 a year at such a job, it would take decades to pay off our debt and that we had no choice but to hang in there. We held hands and prayed together, and from that day forward, we never discussed that option again.

Around that same time, I visited my dad, who was in the habit of walking to church alone near his home several days a week. Come rain or shine, Dad would attend church regularly, despite his disability.

I'll never forget asking Dad why such a devout man as he attended church so frequently. His response was, "Son, I'm not going to church regularly to pray for myself. I'm going to pray for my family, especially for you to find the kind of peace and love for God that I have."

After Dane graduated from high school in 1987, she began college at USL. She worked in restaurants to help pay for school and, in her spare time, helped distribute publications for free,

Dane graduated in 1987 from Chamberlain-Hunt Academy, a Christian military boarding school located in Port Gibson, Miss.

61

never once complaining. She would leave Lafayette after finishing classes for the week and travel to Baton Rouge via New Iberia, Morgan City, Houma and New Orleans, distributing several hundred publications throughout Louisiana's Acadiana region before reaching home late on Friday nights.

From 1984 to 1991, I worked day and night, generating more than 80 percent of all sales for the company. For all practical purposes, I had no full-time sales help until Paul Tyree joined me in the early 1990s. Even though Paul had no formal industrial sales experience, he was, like me, broke and driven to succeed, and we made a great team. The two of us traded for hotel space in Houston for a room that doubled as an office and began rotating our trips so that one of us was in Texas every week.

I firmly believe that in order to win in life, we need good sidekicks and a strong network of folks willing to work together for the betterment of all. As I mentioned earlier, I first learned this in the 1940s and 1950s, when many movie makers stressed the message that good guys win and bad guys lose and that teamwork is the essential component in victory.

This message is just as important today. It rings loud and clear and is repeated time and again throughout this story. After all, to me the definition of "networking" is "getting together to get ahead."

Paul was a classmate of Dane's, as was Harper Jones — both came to work for me at BIC around 1990. Harper stayed for about a year, and Paul was with us until 1996. During that time, two excellent production folks — Mindy Brodhead and Patti Lacobee — used their exceptional editorial and design skills to help build *BIC* into a well-respected publication.

Mindy worked part time until I could afford to hire her as a full-time editor, and Patti worked as a freelance designer. I'll never forget one instance in which Patti hid the material for an issue of the magazine in her oven until Mindy loaned me the money to pay her creative fee (in those days, we often lived on Bodi's salary, as getting a paycheck was never a sure thing for me). Today, Patti is a highly regarded designer in New York, and Mindy is a successful writer with several books to her credit.

As we entered the 1990s, though still deeply in debt, Paul, Bobby Davis, Mindy and I began to turn the company toward success. Bodi was my No. 1 cheerleader. She never complained, and we would never have made it without her. In 1990, Dane married Thomas Brinsko, a law student from Mandeville, La., and transferred to LSU, where Thomas was enrolled. After finishing law school, Thomas went to work for Exxon's land acquisitions division, based in Houston, and Dane completed her edu-

Dane married Thomas Brinsko in 1990. Thomas, pictured here along with his parents, Ada and Thomas Sr., would one day become my partner in the BIC Alliance.

cation at the University of Houston. They worked for BIC in their spare time and played an important role in its success.

On the day Thomas graduated in 1991, adversity struck again — Bodi and I were involved in a near-fatal auto accident. Traveling over 60 mph, a drunk driver hit our vehicle while we were stopped at a red light on Airline Highway in North Baton Rouge. Bodi's foot was crushed, my ribs were broken and the first decent vehicle we'd owned in years was totaled — we'd only had it for two months.

We were faced with another dilemma. Not only was the driver uninsured, but Bodi was now unable to work as a hair stylist, which deprived us of a source of revenue we needed in order to make ends meet.

Since selling our house in 1983, we had lived either in a trailer or an apartment for more than eight years. Thankfully, my wife's parents and my dad came to our rescue. In 1992, Bodi and I scraped together our savings, and Mr. and Mrs. Bodi helped us buy a small house in Baton Rouge. My dad advanced us from his savings three years of royalty revenue from our family's oil property in North Louisiana. For the first time in more than 12 years, we were beginning to see the light at the end of the tunnel. Those experiences taught me that in the absence of money, you should never give up.

Being an underdog and a rebounding entrepreneur myself, I have always tried to help other rebounding entrepreneurs and folks who were similarly down on their luck. Furthermore, the underdog has always been my hero. (Maybe this explains why I am still a New Orleans Saints fan after all these years.)

Just when there was a glimmer of daylight at BIC, I hired a former classmate from Louisiana College who took over as our administrator and chief financial officer. He and his wife were going through a divorce, and I tried to talk her into giving him another chance, to no avail. She told me that I didn't know him the way she did — perhaps I should have taken that as a warning.

One day, about a year later, I was looking for some paper work when I came across a stash of checks for an expensive apartment, in addition to others made out to Baylor University, where the man's daughter was enrolled as a student. Further research revealed that he had been stealing from me from the beginning. (Although he always left enough for me to survive, which he revealed in his confession!)

Thanks to the help of Thomas and my brother, I didn't lose control of my temper.

Like many other times in my life, I tried to look upon this heart-breaking and devastating situation as a learning experience. It taught me that no matter how hard we work, or how devoted we are to our cause, we are only as strong as the people with whom we surround ourselves.

It wasn't until Theresa Kennedy came along in the early '90s that we had a competent financial manager who could help keep the BIC Alliance on a sound financial footing. Theresa was originally hired as an administrative assistant, but eventually worked her way up to her current position as chief financial officer. Today, our company is in excellent financial shape. All of our business and personal real estate is paid for, and we have the financial resources to bankroll expansion without borrowing. (We went for so long with so little that we learned how to operate on cash flow.)

I've seen countless entrepreneurs who spent years trying to reach financial independence, only to begin living the high life at the first taste of success rather than reinvesting in their companies. We took the opposite approach by putting our employees and clients — whom we think of and refer to as partners — first and reinvesting in our people, our databases and the quality of our publications and expanding our distribution and mailings.

The betrayal taught me that we should work only with people who are honest, honorable and willing to work as hard as we do. Furthermore, I realized that we must watch our money with the same diligence and scrutiny with which we should approach sales and the quality of our products and services.

Because I was more hurt than angry, I didn't file formal charges. Instead, with Thomas's help, we worked out a restitution plan for repayment of the stolen money.

Although he never repaid the more than $20,000 he had stolen from me, I learned a valuable lesson that paved the way to the financial success that came years later — there is nothing sadder in the life of a business owner or entrepreneur than employee betrayal.

As I look back over the past 25 years, I can describe the period from 1980 to 1991 only as a time of great adversity — you could say our family got a baptism by fire. We would never have made it had we not turned these great challenges into great adventures.

Without the love of God, loved ones and family and friends in business and industry, we would not have been able to survive and ultimately prosper. I had suffered the loss of precious time with the family I love and all my worldly possessions, and my faith in mankind had been shaken, although I thank God every day that there are more good, honest people in this world than bad, dishonest ones.

But during that 10 years, I had also gained a lifetime of experience in business ethics, sales and marketing, entrepreneurship and networking among peers in business and industry.

Everybody Wins When Movers and Shakers Network

In the early '90s we truly set ourselves apart from every other business or industrial publication in America.

As I mentioned earlier, the essence of the word "team" is captured by the phrase "together, everyone accomplishes more." From that perspective, BIC has been a team effort from day one.

As the BIC Alliance grew across the Gulf Coast and eventually across the United States in the late '80s and early '90s, I had the opportunity to meet many of the most interesting and successful industry executives and entrepreneurs in the oil and gas, construction and environmental industries. I've had the pleasure to learn from some of the best, and they've shared their expertise in management and marketing with me and vice versa.

For our April/May 1990 issue, we featured Buckner Rental in our cover story. Like Oil Mop Founder Wally Landry, who we featured in the 1980s, Robert Buckner considered his business a labor of love. He founded Buckner Rental in 1978, and by the time we met in 1990, he had expanded to nine stores.

Mr. Buckner was the kind of person you would never forget. Having been a national service manager for an equipment company prior to starting Buckner Rental, he could operate and repair every piece of equipment he owned. He believed in diversification — with 50 percent of his business being upstream oil and gas, 25 percent downstream and 20 percent construction, in addition to 5 percent in general household needs. His company was perfect for our publication because his market diversity matched our readership.

Another thing I'll never forget about Mr. Buckner was his straightforwardness. When we first met, he was very outspoken about his thoughts on advertising. Within the first five minutes, he told me that advertising had never worked for him, that he didn't believe in it and, furthermore, he didn't like sharing his success story with others. Instead of being discouraged by his candor, however, I agreed that, like him, I'd had the same experience with advertising prior to launching *BIC*. I explained *BIC*'s uniqueness in combining advertising, editorial content and direct mail.

I went on to say that it was obvious Mr. Buckner placed a high value on his people and the maintenance of his equipment and that perhaps we could feature his managers on the cover and focus on the role their devotion to duty played in his success rather than focusing solely on him. Immediately, Mr. Buckner asked me the investment figure for an annual campaign, and I told him.

His response was, "We spend more than that on caps and T-shirts."

Mr. Buckner's cover story was inspiring in many ways. He believed in what he called the "Midas Touch" when it came to his employees. He demanded excellence, and those not willing to give it their all were not Buckner people for long. Mr. Buckner went on to say that his folks needed all the right stuff — character, loyalty, dedication and a willingness to work beyond the norm. Such qualities aren't created by education or experience, according to Mr. Buckner — they're born from within.

In his interview, he told me that another key to the company's success was to focus its energy on customers to the utmost of its ability instead of worrying about what the competition was doing. Mr. Buckner believed, as I do, that we must set the standards in our chosen industry and let other companies strive to meet them.

Because networking and training were always cornerstones of the BIC Alliance's success, we began sponsoring networking and training events early in our history. We launched Enviro Expo, the first series of industrial-environmental trade shows and conferences ever held in the southern United States. I first got the idea to sponsor this conference after visiting various industrial events, including the Offshore Technology Conference, the LOBOS Industrial Trade Shows and the Environmental Business Conferences, which were being held in Pasadena, Calif., and Boston during the late '80s and early '90s. By 1989, not only were we sponsoring Enviro Expo, we were also sponsoring industry/business conferences in places like Houston, where the first such conference took place, and New Orleans, Baton Rouge and Biloxi, Miss. (We later sponsored another industry/business conference in 1996.)

We'd bring together several hundred industrial executives, plus industrial service entrepreneurs, presidents and CEOs, in addition to upper-level managers in finance, human resources, marketing and sales — featured speakers included Lynn Lantrip of Waste

The BIC Alliance has always promoted networking. At trade shows, conferences and hospitality functions like the one we host during the annual NPRA Reliability & Maintenance Conference and Exhibition, we encourage clients to network with their peers in business and industry. Our hospitality functions are often hosted at hotels that advertise with us, such as the Wyndham New Orleans Hotel at Canal Place, where we held our 2005 event.

Management USA; Browning-Ferris Industries Vice President Marcia Williams; Keith Huber, founder of Keith Huber Inc.; and many others. These events, along with hospitality and networking functions such as the one we currently sponsor during the annual National Petrochemical and Refiners Association (NPRA) Reliability & Maintenance Conference and Exhibition, attracted "who's who" in American industry.

Among the topics and other components of our management and marketing conferences were:

— State of the industry reports.

— Mergers and acquisitions.

— Entrepreneur and executive roundtables.

— Long- and short-range strategies.

— Developing effective marketing and sales tools.

— Strategic marketing and sales.

— Hiring and training the best people.

In 1990, we traveled to Arkansas to do a story on MRK's remote incinerator, the brainchild of a high school friend, Chip Efferson. I also met two men — Clint Pearson and John Egle of Land Treatment Systems, the subjects of our November/December 1990 cover story — who gave me the idea for launching IVS.

From Egle and Pearson, I learned the importance of teaming together partners who compliment one another. Pearson was an expert in finance and law, and Egle's strengths were in operations, sales and marketing.

Another thing I learned from them was the importance of building a company not only to operate, but also to sell if the right opportunity presents itself. Even if we plan to keep a company, running it as though we plan to sell it will prompt us to run it better — i.e. bottom-line orientation, strong organizational chart, etc.

Over the next decade, Egle and I worked to build market share for companies that he either owned or managed. In the early 1980s, Egle had been busy running a Golden Meadow, La., radio station left to his family by his late father. His brother-in-law, who was in the tank cleaning business, asked him to use his contacts to help him find work.

One of the first jobs he generated was one that called for the disposal of 30,000 barrels of production sludge for $5 per barrel, a total of $150,000. Seeing opportunity in the environmental business, Egle, who had been selling radio advertising to small retailers for rates as low as $100 said, "I'm in the wrong business." His subsequent research on the subject led to the discovery of opportunities in the handling of oil field waste, and Land Treatment Systems was born.

Pearson, Egle's attorney, left his law practice, and, together, they approached B.I. Moody and Tom Becnel of Lafayette, La., who agreed to capitalize additional treatment cells at the Land Treatment Systems site south of Morgan City, La.

During the late 1980s and early 1990s, we began conducting several public relations and awareness programs for Star Enterprises in Beaumont, Texas, and Texaco Chemical Company's Port Neches, Texas, plant.

Our relationship with industrial corporations and service companies has grown better over the years because they have important messages they need to share with their employees, stakeholders, the community and with regulators and legislators locally, regionally and nationally, and we help them in many different ways. For instance, each time we sign a marketing agreement, we add the names of our new partners' clients and prospects to our mailing list and send them complimentary subscriptions of *BIC* and *TLC* on behalf of the new partners. (All of our partners are given the opportunity to cherrypick our mailing lists for up to 800 names per year.) Additionally, we add the names of trade show and conference attendees, association members and paid subscribers.

BIC's database is now considered by many in industry as the country's best — a veritable "who's who" of American industry.

By the end of 1990, Enviro Expo had evolved into one of the most important environmental events in the southern United States, with attendees, speakers and exhibitors traveling from all across North America to participate. More than 1,000 attendees and 100 exhibitors participated in our Enviro Expo in Kenner, La., in the spring of 1992.

By far, our largest public relations and employee relations campaign during that time involved a comic strip character by the name of Captain Wow ("Wow" stood for "War on Waste"). The campaign took place at Star Enterprises' Port Arthur, Texas, Refinery and was featured in our January/February 1991 issue. This program, which we had helped launch in 1990, created environmental awareness throughout Southeast Texas, as Captain Wow took his war on waste to thousands of children each year. The management and staff of Star Enterprises and the Texaco Chemical Plant in nearby Port Neches were great to work with. They helped build the reputation of the BIC Alliance as an industry communications partner that is still alive and well today.

Another major marketing and public relations project took place in 1988 during the Republican National Convention in New Orleans, when we added an extra 15,000 copies to our printing for distribution of *BIC* in host hotels. Featured company Marine Shale Processing, which was owned by Jack Kent at the time, wanted to get its message to America's top-ranking Republicans, and the convention offered the perfect opportunity to reach them all at once. (What's more, the cover of the issue we distributed featured prominent Republican lobbyist Fred Thompson, who went on to serve in the U.S. Senate and act in major motion pictures and the TV series

Law & Order.)

I volunteered to work on the group that helped round up Louisiana products to put in the VIP and media promotional packets so that I could include *BIC* among the "goodies." A team from the BIC Alliance worked all night to achieve further distribution objectives. Around midnight, I cut my finger while reaching for a stack of magazines and had to have six stitches to close the wound. After my visit to the emergency room, I returned to distributing *BIC*, and we completed our task around dawn.

Following that successful marketing and PR campaign, we got calls from firms across America wanting to learn more about the BIC Alliance and our marketing techniques. We had truly set ourselves apart from every other business or industrial publication in America.

Around that time I read an excellent book titled, *Guerrilla Marketing*, and got some great new ideas that we would soon integrate into our operations. However, when I thought of the term "guerrilla marketing," I couldn't help but think of a gorilla pounding on its chest and making a loud roar.

To me, sales and marketing is about listening and strategic planning. I named our marketing techniques and, later, my seminars and keynote presentations, "Alligator Management & Marketing" because the alli-

During my Alligator Management & Marketing seminars, I share a wide variety of management, marketing and sales techniques, including tips on networking, prospecting, closing and professional etiquette, and what I call "listening for success."

73

gator is as quiet as a mouse — until it strikes. Furthermore, the alligator has no vocal cords and has survived since prehistoric times because it is a great listener.

As I stress in my Alligator Management & Marketing seminars, there are two types of managers and sales folks — those who are interested and those who are interesting. The interested are the most successful. Why? Because they are listening instead of talking. Perhaps that's why God gave us two ears and one mouth — so we'd listen twice as much as we talk. I've studied non-verbal communication for years, and I truly enjoy sharing such techniques in my seminars.

(On a more personal level, Alligator Management & Marketing is named so because the animal is a symbol of the Louisiana heritage we at the BIC Alliance hold dear.)

Among our largest marketing partners between 1990 and 1993 were Rollins; Plant Machine Works; Charles Holston Inc.; Separation Systems Consultants Inc. (SSCI); The Cajun Crusher; Walk, Haydel and Associates.; LOBOS; Basic Industries Petroleum; Geraghty and Miller; and SGB — an international scaffolding company run by Neil Woods and my good friend David Starkey.

David and I became friends during the days when I'd leave my car running while on sales calls so I wouldn't have to jumpstart it when I left (I couldn't afford an alternator). Today, David is one of the owners of Empire Scaffold and one of the longest-running of all our marketing partners.

The July 1991 issue of *BIC* was sponsored by Laidlaw, whose CEO at the time was Bill Stillwell. Bill was a great guy to work with and spoke at several of our Enviro Expos and industrial entrepreneurs' conferences. Our March/April 1992 issue was sponsored by C. M. Penn, which sold its trucking division to Gulf South Systems (the latter company went on to sell that division to CEI

Environmental Services in the late '90s in a deal that enhanced the growth of the BIC Alliance and IVS).

The 1990s were called the "Decade of the Environment," and that's when *BIC* became the publication of choice for industrial, construction and environmental decision makers. During that period, the environmental industry was growing by leaps and bounds. I traveled to Los Angeles, Boston and Washington to learn about growth opportunities and also learn how to successfully market environmental manufacturing and service companies. The adverse things we had done to our environment for decades created job opportunities for tens of thousands and business opportunities for hundreds in construction and industrial engineering. In that number, I was one who, once again, turned adversity into opportunity.

When the Valdez oil spill took place in 1989, I was in the right place at the right time. The incident created a great opportunity for emergency response businesses to create top-of-mind awareness in industry. We helped turn the adverse publicity that resulted from the Valdez spill into an opportunity for ourselves and our clients in the emergency response and environmental businesses, and *BIC*, which already had a heavy emphasis on safety and the environment, went on to become a great success and expanded at the national level.

By the beginning of 1993, not only had we changed the name of the publication from the *Business and Industry Coordinator* to the *Business and Industry Connection*, we had also

Our company was incorporated as the Business and Industry Communications (BIC) Alliance in 1992 in order to position it as the primary network for buyers and sellers in business and industry.

75

evolved into the premier industrial and environmental marketing firm in the southern United States. The BIC Alliance helped launch more industrial and environmental companies and new industrial technology than any other trade publication during that period.

Early in the year, I had met and become a marketing partner with one of the early pioneers of environmental manufacturing — Will Crenshaw of Modern Manufacturing in Beaumont, Texas. Since 1961, Modern Manufacturing had provided good quality equipment manufacturing capability. The BIC Alliance was chosen to help market and promote Modern's Dragon Gut™ waste containers, and the company became our largest marketing partner until its environmental rental division was sold a few years later. I loved working with Will and his entire family. He believes not only in building the best equipment in the industry, but also in being the leader in the marketing of environmental, industrial and oil field equipment. Modern became the corporate sponsor for Enviro Expo and sponsored more front and back covers than any company before it. We developed a great marketing partnership and a mutual respect that remains alive and well today. (Will's sons Casey and Colby have since joined him at Modern and are following in his footsteps in delivering quality products that are aggressively marketed.)

During 1993, we had many other great companies join the BIC Alliance and/or renew their marketing campaigns. Two of my most loyal and supportive partners were Claude Barber of Plant Machine Works and Ronnie Reynerson (now deceased) of Appco. Claude often pre-paid me in order to help cover printing and mailing expenses, and Ronnie helped distribute more copies of *BIC* than any other partner in our history. Every two weeks, Ronnie would stop by our office and pick up several hundred copies of *BIC*. He would apply to them his own trademark label, which indicated the page numbers of his ads and editorial copy, and hand them out to industrial facilities across the southern United States.

In January 1993, I traveled to Little Rock, Ark., to distribute *BIC* during President Clinton's economic summit prior to his taking office. On that trip I also met Herb Kelleher, president and CEO of Southwest Airlines, whom I later visited in Dallas to hear his story of entrepreneurship. *BIC* was the only business or industry trade publication that was distributed at the airports and hotels during that economic summit.

"Bonus" distribution at trade shows and conferences became an added feature of our strategic marketing programs that expanded every year. Many of our front covers are chosen by companies such as Hertz Equipment Rental, which has taken the front cover for the month of the CON-EXPO show, and Brock Enterprises, which is normally featured during the month of the NPRA Reliability & Maintenance Conference and Exhibition, because of this unique feature. We believed then, as we do now, that in order to be America's leader in industrial and environmental publications, we needed to offer much more than great advertising, editorial and direct marketing. If we were to be a leader, we needed to be the most widely read publication when and where leaders gathered. By the end of 1993, we were participants in over a dozen trade shows and conferences annually from coast to coast. Currently, *BIC* and *TLC* are bonus distributed at more than 30 trade shows a year from coast to coast.

Over the past 25 years, Bodi and I, along with our staff, have traveled hundreds of thousands of miles distributing our publications at trade shows, conferences and forced-waiting areas across America.

Many times in the dead of winter and in 100-plus-degree summers, my cars would break down from the weight of magazines as I traveled across the South distributing publications. During my hitchhiking days, when cars would pass me in the pouring rain or freezing cold, part of my dream was to own a fleet of Lincolns as a calling card for the successful business I would one day own and manage. This dream was kept alive by the many dilapidated cars and trucks I had to drive on my journey to success. After years of hard work and sacrifice, the dream was realized during the 10th anniversary of our business in 1994.

After buying my first pre-owned Lincoln in 1994, I drove it on a sales call in New Orleans during a heavy rain. As I checked on the car before going to bed that night, it was up to its headlights in water. Nevertheless, I was convinced that not even flooding could dampen my dreams.

However, a few months after buying that first ("pre-owned," not used) Lincoln, I drove it on a sales call in New Orleans during a downpour. As I checked on the car before going to bed that night, it was up to its headlights in water. Nevertheless, I was convinced that not even flooding could dampen my dream.

Now, each time I walk up to one of my company's Lincolns, I am reminded of the hard road we have traveled, I'm reminded of those days when hitchhiking was a necessity, and I'm reminded of the cars and trucks that sputtered out and had to be fixed along the way.

I'm also reminded of all those who helped me get around by

providing me with transportation — Jimmy Culpepper, Mike Conners, Bobby Davis, "Big" Ernie Hernandez, Thomas Heard and Gerry Lane, owner and operator of Gerry Lane Enterprises, who in the late 1980s allowed me to apply his advertising investment as a down payment toward the first new vehicle I'd owned in years.

Bobby Davis, my high school friend and long-time BICster, was one of many who helped us make it through our darkest hours.

How We Die is More Important than How We Live

No matter how hard things may become
or how little we might have, we simply must
stop periodically to take a break.

From 1990 to 1995, we refined *BIC* by expanding into all facets of energy and into pulp and paper and power generation. By 1990, we were poised for growth, and we spent the next five years becoming debt free and building a reputation as America's largest multi-industry, multi-departmental newsmagazine. We had learned how to build something out of nothing but hard work, perseverance and a savvy marketing formula that we loved to share with others.

However, one of the most important things I learned from those days is that, no matter how hard things may become or how little we might have, we simply must put family first and stop periodically to take a break. I began learning this painful lesson during my first business venture and the period from 1983 to 1987, when working was about all I did.

There is an old saying that the fruit doesn't fall far from the tree. Not only were Bodi's parents and mine among the hardest workers I have ever met, but they also believed in spending quality spare time with loved ones. From the earliest years of our lives, our parents had placed a high value on wholesome leisure time activities. Both our parents had owned camps at False River for years, and Bodi, Dane, Thomas, our grandchildren and I have cherished the memories we've made while fishing, boating and camping out on weekends and during holidays.

Even though Bodi and I went many years without a real vacation, we went to False River every chance we got to rest, relax and prepare physically and mentally for the challenges ahead. In the poorest of times, we used our families' camps and boats and rarely dined out, except at restaurants where we had bartered for marketing services, advertising, etc.

Often times while camping out, I'd awaken in the wee hours of the morning and spend several hours thinking and planning strategy for the days, weeks and months ahead. I loved drinking coffee, watching sunrises and sunsets, and spending those precious hours in nature with loved ones.

During the early 1990s, Bodi and I found an old, dilapidated camp about midway between those of our parents, rented it for $85 per month and agreed to restore it to a livable condition. Thanks again to my carpentry skills, in concert with help from family, friends, co-workers and lots of duct tape, we patched the place together.

Most of the dreams and plans for our future were conceived and refined on the back porch and pier of that camp, just as they had been in that nearby trailer 10 years earlier. By

During the early '90s, Bodi and I found an old, dilapidated camp midway between those of our parents and restored it to a livable condition.

1995, Bodi and I were strong enough financially to buy a large home in Baton Rouge and a second home on the banks of False River near New Roads — great timing, as our first grandchild, Hannah Yvonne Brinsko, was born on June 22 of that year.

Both my parents and Bodi's told us decades ago that one of the greatest joys you can experience in life is owning a home that's paid for. Since the early '90s, Bodi and I have used what we call the "stair-step approach" to home ownership. In the beginning, we

81

saved our money and bought a small home we could afford to pay for in cash. Next, we saved some more and stepped up to the next notch. It took four steps and 12 years for us to finally acquire the home of our dreams, which is located on a beautiful lake in Baton Rouge.

We visit the bayous and coastlines of our beloved Louisiana as often as possible and enjoy brainstorming for ideas for upcoming issues of *BIC* and *TLC* and what adventures we have yet to experience. *TLC* was conceived along the bank of False River, as had been the case previously with IVS, our merger and acquisition and executive recruiting company. I'm not sure why, but there is something about being around nature — water, in particular — that seems to elevate creative thinking to new heights. Somehow, the solitude of nature and participation in golf, fishing and other relaxing outdoor activities seems to allow our minds to think in a three-dimensional way, enabling us to come up with better solutions to problems.

Show me a person who doesn't take a break, and I'll show you a person who will never be able to compete as effectively or be as successful in his or her business and family life as the person who does.

Today, Bodi and I enjoy the privilege of sitting on our back porch and enjoying nature at its best, watching sunrises and sunsets that are as beautiful to us as the view from the South rim of the Grand Canyon or the majestic, snow-covered mountains of Alaska.

The year 1996 was one of the saddest and most challenging of my life. My dad, who had become my best friend since my mom's death in 1986, died that year. After having caused my parents much sadness when my first business failed in 1981, one of the greatest joys of my life was rebuilding this wonderful relationship with my dad. Thankfully, he lived long enough to see Bodi and me begin to turn the corner in both our business and spiritual lives and Hannah's birth.

The adversity I had found and the disappointment I had caused

82

family and friends inspired Bodi and me to strive for success in our business, personal and spiritual lives or die trying. Dad, Bodi, Dane and Thomas were my greatest cheerleaders, and I thank God that Dad lived to see us nearly debt free, with our own home and office building, sharing God's message of love with others. In addition, no one prayed harder for us than Bodi's sister Beverly, who passed away in 2004 after a gallant and inspiring bout with cancer, and my dad. Both Beverly and Dad believed, as do Bodi and I, that God placed us in the communications and training business for a purpose.

Even at his death, my dad — commonly known as "Mr. Leo" because he was so well-respected — was an inspiration to our entire family and everyone who knew him. There never seemed to be any doubt in his mind nor in the minds of those of us who knew him that he was going to heaven to be with God and loved ones who had gone before him.

Bodi and I always referred to my dad as the perfect Southern gentleman, and no truer words were ever spoken. Of course, like most loving wives, she always encourages me to be more like my dad and other Southern gentlemen in my faith and demeanor. After more than 40 years as my soulmate and best friend, she reports that I am making great progress! Thank God for the guidance of wives, family members and friends who aren't afraid to help guide us along life's path.

When the doctors told us that Dad wasn't going to make it, my brother, sister and I were devastated. After breaking the news to us, the doctor entered Dad's room to tell him just after the hospital attendant had delivered his evening meal. After the doctor left, my brother, sister and I entered the room somber and saddened, with tears in our eyes.

None of us knew what to say or how to act. My brother George, in a gallant effort to lift our spirits, asked Dad if he would like more of his partially eaten supper before it got cold. My dad, with a twinkle in his eye and a smile across his face, said in a loving voice, "No, son, the doctor seems to have ruined my appetite."

I'll never forget my dad's actions as he took our hands, held them tightly and said, "Looks like I'm going home." Even in the hours before his death, Dad demonstrated his faith in God by helping to bring peace to others. He was a gentle, God-loving man who showed us how to die with style. He had absolutely no fear of death because he had the peace of knowing that he was going to a better place.

Folks, over the past 60 years, I've learned great lessons from some of the most successful people in America, but none more precious than the one I learned that night from my dad — how we live is important, but how we die is far more important.

Dad held our hands that night and prayed that we would always be close on Earth and, one day, reunited in heaven. Seeing his peace and happiness in both life and death has played a tremendous role in my spiritual journey.

My dad and Beverly shared another thing in common — they both inspired Bodi and me to make God first in our lives and share God's love for others in what we say and do. Around 1987, Bodi and I had begun to attend church more and pray regularly. It was then that Bible reading became one of my greatest joys. The Gideons did the world a great service when they put Bibles in hotel rooms around the nation — on hundreds of occasions, I've read the good book's stories of faith, love and perseverance during the sleepless nights of work- and leisure-related trips. It's now something that I do regularly in times of stress and challenge for the pure joy it brings me and for the lessons it teaches me.

What Doesn't Kill You Makes You Stronger

---

*It is always darkest just
before the dawn.*

Paul Tyree was offered a sales management position with AllService, a BIC Alliance marketing partner in Texas, in 1996. His departure was bittersweet for all of us because he and I had become a great team, and his contributions helped get the BIC Alliance on a sound financial footing. Even though Paul was no longer a full-time "BICster," we continued to have an excellent relationship. It remains so to this day.

In 1997, with Paul's help, IVS (then known as Ind-Viro Marketing) was the intermediary firm that helped facilitate the acquisition of AllService by Total Safety.

Matt Malatesta, a Texan who graduated from the Manship School of Mass Communication at LSU, took over management of our Western U.S. operations in Houston

Ind-Viro Search, the BIC Alliance's merger and acquisition and executive recruiting firm, helps industrial leaders hire the right people and links buyers and sellers of major companies.

— which had opened in 1995 — and played an important role in the continued growth of the BIC Alliance and IVS. During his time at the BIC Alliance, Matt set sales appointments for me, wrote columns for *BIC*, handled our newly founded creative services division and learned how to sell. He published his first novel, *It's*

My Life, a story about a Texas high school football team, in 2004.

Upon completion of the acquisition of AllService, Bodi and I reinvested the entire intermediary fee into changing the cover of *BIC* to a glossy format. Although the fee covered the printing for only four of our 12 annual front covers, we were convinced that this strategic move would be a wise one.

It was around this time that our dear friend Ralph Hay of Dixie Web passed away.

Not long after his death, we entered partnerships with Baker Printing of Baker, La., led by Andy Bishop and his family, and Baton Rouge Press, which is owned by Pat Prather. The former now prints all of our covers and the latter prints the body of each magazine we produce. Each does an excellent job, and our continued success could not have been possible without their hard work and dedication.

By the end of the four issues, our sales had increased well beyond the amount needed to cover the increased printing investment. Notice that I say "investment" instead of "cost." We believe strongly that one should develop the mindset that taking action to better market or grow his or her company is an investment, not a cost.

When an owner is confident enough to invest in his/her own company, it helps build confidence in that company among its partners and customers. We invested every dollar we had and borrowed hundreds of thousands more, feeling confident that we were truly going the extra mile.

One of the things I've found most interesting about the most successful entrepreneurs and business executives is that money is rarely their primary driving force.

Most, including myself, really enjoy what we do and would probably do it for free if we could. Another observation I find interesting is that once we have reached tremendous success or are starting to reach it, we continue to derive greater peace and happiness from helping others in the process. Furthermore, I firmly believe that the notion that "givers get" is totally true.

When you're doing what you have to do and you're doing the best you can to serve those who invest in your company's products and/or services, good things tend to happen. One of those good things is financial success. As Mr. Andre had told me 30 years earlier, the key to success in business is to stay in business. Hang in there! Good employees will come and go, but if you're doing a good job, the business they helped generate will stay with you.

Along the way, we've had some great folks who've been part of the BIC Alliance — some as marketing partners, some as employees and tens of thousands who've been loyal readers. Like any successful company, we've lost some great folks along the way, but other great folks have taken their places.

Life, it seems, is a journey of hills and valleys. While 1996 was a year of great challenge and adversity, 1997 was our best year in business since our inception. As they say, it is always darkest just before the dawn. In the case of the BIC Alliance, no truer words were ever spoken.

Paul's departure inspired me and everyone who remained at the BIC Alliance to work harder and to do what had to be done to sustain our growth. What took place over the course of the next year reminded me of the old Gene Autry song, "Back in the Saddle Again." In 1997, I got back in the saddle and took over the reins — not only in sales, but also in production. That year, I traveled about 100 days, mostly in Texas, but also nationally whenever the situation dictated.

Thankfully, Theresa Kennedy and Kathy Hayward, our production manager — along with our entire staff — did an excellent job in Louisiana. With the help of Matt in Texas and Chris Coffee in Louisiana, not to mention the glossy cover change, we grew by about 20 percent in 1997. In his own way of saying "job well done," Sonny Anderson, my benefactor, who co-signed a note to keep the BIC Alliance alive in the mid 1980s, sponsored one of our front covers that year.

Chris Pettitt, who worked for us as an account executive from 1997 to 2003, played an important role in the growth of both *BIC* and IVS, and helped spur the growth of our Western U.S. operations. Chris, along with IVS independent agent Billy Gauthier, helped initiate our intermediary role in CEI Environmental Services' 1998 acquisition of Gulf South Systems' transportation division, one of the largest deals in the history of IVS.

Bodi and I continued to live comfortably and to devote all extra revenue to expansion and to paying off debt. By 1997, we were almost debt free, and we celebrated by paying off the building we had agreed to lease-purchase several years earlier (it remains to this day our corporate headquarters). It had taken 14 years to fulfill our financial obligations and to begin reaping the fruits of our labor.

In the latter part of the decade, several things happened that not only changed my life, but also altered the course of the BIC Alliance forever. One of our biggest business moves was to stop producing the Enviro Expo trade shows and focus all our attention on our flagship publication and executive recruiting and merger and acquisition activities.

During that period, Thomas, who was in the prime of a successful career with Key Production (now Cimarex Energy Co.) in New Orleans, began to show great interest in joining me in running the BIC Alliance. For years, Thomas had written a column for *BIC*, and both he and Dane had joined Bodi and me at key industry related events, i.e. trade shows, conferences, networking functions, etc.

Bodi and I had always dreamed and prayed that someday Dane and Thomas would join us in taking the BIC Alliance into the 21st century. However, we all wanted to be sure that the timing and circumstances were right before any changes were made.

Ill health had not been among the many trials I'd endured in my life up to that point. However, in April 1998, just prior to leaving for the Industrial Fire World show in Houston, I began to suffer from chest pains. Bodi insisted that, instead of leaving for Texas, I should go to the hospital. She may have saved my life, as I was, in fact, experiencing heart problems and had to undergo angioplasty to re-establish good circulation. Of course, this also meant a change in lifestyle, regular medication, exercise and a reduced work load.

However, this was a minor setback compared to that which had occurred in August 1997.

I was on one of my regular visits to Houston when I was car-jacked at gunpoint by three men who beat me into unconsciousness, robbed me and left me for dead near Interstate 10.

As I felt the cold steel of a gun being pressed against my head, it seemed as though every breath I took would be my last. However, the angels were with me that night — I believe the only reason my attackers didn't shoot me was because they thought they had beaten me to death.

From the moment I was attacked, my first thoughts were of God and my family.

Bleeding profusely, I feared that I would die before making it to the hospital. It took almost three hours for me to get stitched up and for the MRI to be conducted to see if there had been permanent brain damage. The doctor reassured me, however, by telling me that I was a hard-headed Cajun.

During my struggle to maintain consciousness and get to a hospital, and later while getting stitched up, I repeatedly thanked God for sparing me and promised to Him that I'd devote the rest of my life to being a better Christian and a better person and to share His message of love and forgiveness with others — writing this book was a part of that vow.

I also vowed once again to spend more quality time with my wonderful family — which soon became one bigger with the addition of our second granddaughter, Mary Ada Brinsko, born Feb. 20, 1998 — and to devote more time and resources to helping others learn how to find greater peace, happiness and success by putting God first in their lives. I truly believe God saved my life that August night because He had a greater purpose ahead for me.

During my recuperation period I reflected upon the times in my life when my dream of becoming an entrepreneur was figuratively carjacked, beaten senseless and left for dead by those who, for one reason or another, tried to kill my aspirations. But if you are to be a successful entrepreneur, neither debt, nor ill health, or any other major setback can be allowed to deter you from reaching your goal. This formula is key to anyone seeking success in his or her business or personal life. Your will and your faith in God must be as durable as the hide of the reptile, from which my Alligator Management & Marketing program gets its name.

Just as in the words of the Sly & the Family Stone anthem, "You Can Make It If You Try," you too can succeed by making a solid effort fueled by passion and resolve.

After these life-altering experiences, not only did I decide to devote more time to sharing God's message with others and more quality time with my family, Bodi and I decided that we needed more strong Christian leadership to help take BIC into the new century.

Our prayers were answered in April 1999 when Thomas, along with Dane, decided to leave his job with Key Production to become my partner in the BIC Alliance. They moved from Mandeville to Baton Rouge in the summer of 1999 and bought a home just down the street from us, making Bodi and I delirious with happiness. Thomas and Dane were excited about joining the BIC Alliance, and our beautiful grandchildren, Hannah and Mary, were in Baton Rouge for our entire family to enjoy even more.

My son-in-law and partner Thomas joined the BIC Alliance in 1999 and was promoted to president and chief operating officer in 2002.

Keeping On Keeping On

The BIC Alliance continued to grow by leaps and bounds as we entered the 21st century.

With the Holy Spirit's guidance, Thomas and I — aided by a great staff and marketing partners and our loyal readers — steered the BIC Alliance to unprecedented growth. Within a few years of joining the company in 1999, Thomas had learned all facets of the administration, production and sales management of *BIC*. Prior to his arrival, *BIC* was perceived primarily as an advertorial publication with only a few features. However, Thomas's hard work and emphasis on quality editorial (including more industry news, technical articles, etc.) brought *BIC* to greater respectability. He was promoted to president and chief operating officer of the BIC Alliance and IVS in 2002.

From 1996 to 2004, not only did the annual readership of our publications increase from approximately 650,000 readings to more than 1.5 million, but the BIC Alliance also doubled in sales and expanded at the national level. Although *BIC* began as a Louisiana publication, nowadays only 30 percent of our business comes out of our home state, with 40 percent being done in Texas and the other 30 percent nationwide. (On a side note, I have known Kathleen Babineaux Blanco, Louisiana's current governor, and Lt. Gov. Mitch Landrieu for more than 20 years, having met them when they were members of the state legislature. Gov. Blanco and Lt. Gov. Landrieu are two of the hardest working, most dedicated officials the state has had in years and both are working diligently to promote economic development and tourism worldwide for Louisiana. We at the BIC Alliance take great pride in helping share the good news about Louisiana and the Gulf South with the rest of the world and appreciate others in state and local government and the role these folks and others across the South have played in our efforts.)

Louisiana Governor Kathleen Babineaux Blanco is one of the hardest-working, most dedicated officials the state has had in years, as is Lieutenant Governor Mitch Landrieu. We appreciate their efforts and enjoy working with them and others across the Gulf South to promote economic development and tourism.

The BIC Alliance continued to grow by leaps and bounds as we entered the 21st century. Due to the excellent work of our production team and input from our knowledgeable sales staff, the content of our flagship publication became more informative and insightful with each issue.

The tragic and disturbing events of Sept. 11, 2001, and the demise of corporations such as Enron in 2002 presented many challenges not only for the American public but also for industry, as security and stability became the issues of the day. Although it seemed as though corporate integrity was at a premium in 2002, as I peruse the pages of our publications from that year, I am reminded that there are still honest, hard working men of virtue leading corporations in all sectors of industry. Just by reading their insights into personal success and the empowerment of others, I can see clearly why we as a nation have been able to bounce back from the events of 9/11 and stand united in the face of adversity. (When I think of the Civil War and all that I've read and heard about it since early childhood, it amazes me how our great nation was once so divided, and I thank God that today we are truly the *United* States of

America.)

The year 2002 was a big one for the BIC Alliance and its partners. January marked the biggest month in terms of membership growth we'd ever had. Also, our June issue marked the first time in our history that we sponsored a back cover in our own publication, as we explained how we can help connect the right people and the right companies through IVS. In the accompanying story, we illustrated how IVS had used its matchmaking expertise to locate qualified candidates for positions with companies such as Kiebler-Thompson and Kenny Industrial Services; assisted CEI Environmental Services in purchasing Gulf South Systems' transportation division; helped build AllService; and assisted in the sale of AllService to Total Safety.

Since launching *BIC* in 1984, we'd always had many hospitality and high-end leisure partners who wanted to reach our readers on both the regional and national levels. In 2002, as part of our commitment to putting the betterment of mankind first in our lives, we initiated plans to launch *The Leisure Connection*, which had long been a section in *BIC*, as a stand-alone publication. I wanted a wholesome, family-oriented leisure publication with a heavy emphasis on off-the-job safety, since more people get hurt off the job than on. Additionally, since it seemed that most people enjoyed several types of leisure activities, just like my own family, I wanted *TLC* to be a multi-leisure publication that would open the door to many kinds of family- and work-related adventures.

In the research we conducted prior to publishing *TLC*, we found that baby boomers were retiring earlier and that unlike their parents — many of whom had lived through the Great Depression, worked longer and were more frugal — they enjoyed more of the finer things in life. This led us to believe that there were excellent business opportunities in what we refer to as the "indulgence" market.

Not only that, the Gulf South region ranks highly with regard to tourism and the variety of convention and meeting destinations available. Our mission for *TLC* was to help our readers from the Gulf South enjoy their home in addition to helping bring others from across America to the region.

Using *BIC's* success formula, we launched *TLC* in July 2002 as a multi-leisure, multi-state publication. With *TLC* as the foundation, we then had a vehicle to launch an event planning division and to offer getaway packages such as hunting and fishing trips, golf outings and hotel stays. By becoming our publication's biggest client, we truly became marketing partners with our other advertisers. That formula sounds simple today, but it took decades to refine it and use it

The Leisure Connection began as an insert in BIC and became a stand-alone publication in July 2002.

in the most effective way — the rapid success of *TLC* truly underscored that achievement. As the publication grew, we began to feature in it more meeting coordination and event planning articles, along with more safety, community service and spirituality-related features and executive- and entrepreneur-at-leisure interviews.

Whether we keep *TLC* as a stand-alone publication and a section in *BIC* or just the latter, the final decision will be determined by our readers and partners. Regardless of what route we take, we will always strongly emphasize through our editorial wholesome living; safety both on the job and off; and the community service activities of organizations in business and industry.

The true highlight of 2002, however, was the birth of our first grandson — Thomas Michael Brinsko III. As fate would have it, little Michael shares his birthday (Oct. 16) with his dad and paternal granddad.

The following year was marked by transition. During the summer, Thomas and Dane offered to relocate to Houston in order to expand our operations in the Western U.S. with new regional sales manager and native Texan Terry Grover after the departure of Chris Pettitt. (This meant that Bodi would be accompanying me on almost every trip I would take to Houston in order to spend as much time with Dane, Thomas and our grandchildren as possible!)

Although the changes were challenging for our family, I can say with pride that what took place that year has taken the BIC Alliance to a new level. With many industrial companies feeling the adverse effects of geopolitical instability (the most prominent factor being the Iraq war), some of our marketing partners faced an uphill battle. We wanted to be there to help, and I'm happy to report that many of our advertisers had banner years.

At the beginning of 2004, our company resolved to never stop learning and to pass whatever knowledge we'd gain over to our readers. That summer, our team traveled to Valero's St. Charles facility in Norco, La., to attend the "Refining Basics Academy" and increase our knowledge of the industry. Judging by their commitment to safety, teamwork, community service, environmental stewardship and perseverance, we were confident that the Valero team would be more than qualified to educate us, and they were. (Ron Guillory, with whom I'd worked at Hill Petroleum in 1982, had become a human resources manager for Valero and helped coordinate our visit.)

Not only did we learn more about the process of refining, we also enabled ourselves to closely examine key issues facing the petroleum and chemical industries and draw our own conclusions as to how they could be resolved, making the *BIC* newsmagazine the best it's ever been.

Here at the BIC Alliance, I can certainly say that our people have made us successful throughout our 20-plus years, and it was all because we made a commitment long ago to hire the best folks available — and to feed our minds with new and helpful information.

By the nature of our business, many folks have not only honed their management, sales, marketing and operations experience at the BIC Alliance, they've also built a network of contacts that opened the door to what they felt were greater business or entrepreneurship opportunities elsewhere.

In the case of Kathy Hayward, we helped her pursue her entrepreneurial dreams by selling her our interest in Sulfuric Acid Today and helping finance the acquisition of a publication we had helped launch with her present partner, Jack Harris. Similarly, Paul Tyree, Matt Malatesta, Chris Pettitt and others honed their management and sales skills at BIC and made contacts who helped them become successful in their future endeavors.

God has blessed Thomas and I in that every time an employee has moved on, another person has come along and helped us to grow. And, even better, some have stayed the course and have made the BIC Alliance part of their long-term career plans. Among those who have come and stayed are Bobby Davis, who's been with us since our inception; Theresa Kennedy; *BIC* Editorial Director Jamie Craig and Production Director Heather Abboud, who joined us in 1997 and 1999, respectively; and others. I credit Thomas for not only helping to improve the *BIC* newsmagazine, build its reputation and get better results for our partners, but also for drawing excellent people to our company who are proud to have joined an organization that treats each staff member like a partner.

Here at the BIC Alliance, we're trainers and communicators first and foremost. We believe and have proved that we can train good people to be great and great people to be phenomenal. Perhaps this explains the success of IVS — we're so adept at training the right people to do the right jobs that we know both when we see them (not to mention our ability to match buyers and sellers, another skill honed from years of connecting business and industry with one another through strategic marketing).

Among the phenomenal individuals who are currently helping to further the success of the BIC Alliance and maintain it through the 21st century are our administrative and customer relations staff, which includes Theresa Kennedy, Kathy Dugas MacMenamin, Bobby Davis, Jon Guillaume,

Here at the BIC Alliance, we believe and have proved that we can train good people to be great and great people to be phenomenal. The BIC family is shown here enjoying our 2004 Christmas party.

Brooke Nelson and Sherry Ferrell; our sales team — Terry Grover, Joe Storer, Jeremy Osterberger and Lance LeBlanc; and our production staff — Heather Abboud, Jamie Craig, Denise Poché, Kaye Benham, Brady Porche, Katie Macaluso and Susan Pickens.

In September 2004, we retained Mike Bourgeois, a semi-retired, award-winning public relations professional known to our readers as a columnist for *BIC* and *TLC*, and enlisted the help of Brady Porche, editor-in-chief of *TLC*, to assist in the writing and publication of this book as a pilot project for the possible establishment and addition of a book publishing operation to the BIC Alliance family.

Every day, we're writing new chapters — not only in our lives, but in the ever-evolving story of the BIC Alliance as well.

What's Ahead for the BIC Alliance?

We are expanding our role not only as America's, but also the world's, business and industry connection.

As we forge ahead, we thank God for blessing us with a wonderful staff, great marketing partners and loyal readers who respond to our requests for interviews and articles for *BIC* and help us to determine what additional products and services we should offer.

During the coming years, we will travel from coast to coast, partnering in trade shows and conferences, where we will bonus distribute our publications and our industry event calendar — the *BIC Planner* — which highlights several industry and business trade shows and conferences across America.

Our annual industry event calendar, the BIC Planner, is the most in-depth trade show and conference listing in the energy and construction industries.

In recent years, *BIC* has expanded all across America and is read in every state. Our Web sites, www.bicalliance.com, www.bicpublishing.com and www.theleisureconnection.net, are getting hits from around the world. Recently, my good friend Bud Howard and I visited via telephone while he was on an international business trip for Volvo. Bud was reviewing the most recent news on our Web site and inquired about recent merger and acquisition activity, proving to me that the world is becoming more connected, and that we are expanding our role not only as America's, but also the world's, business and industry connection.

As for IVS, we're getting calls from around the country from folks interested in buying or selling their companies or utilizing our recruiting services. We've recently placed several high-level executives and managers and currently have more than six IVS merger and acquisition activities at various levels of negotiation.

Thomas has taken over the day-to-day operations of the BIC Alliance. He has devoted himself to continuously improving not only our editorial and marketing capabilities, but our database as well. Thanks to his efforts, many of our marketing partners think we've got the best multi-industry database and prospecting tools in America. During the past few years, we've added almost 5,000 new names, not only in the petroleum industry, but in pulp and paper and power generation as well. The top marketing and sales executives among our BIC Alliance partners travel regularly to our offices in Texas and Louisiana for strategic marketing planning sessions and to cherrypick our database for names of qualified prospects.

In the months and years to come, we'll be announcing new merger and acquisition partnerships, expanding our management and sales training capability and will have published this, the first book in what we hope will be a series about successful individuals, organizations and associations in industry and business. (In 2006, if all goes as planned, we may even host a business and industry conference similar to events we conducted in 1989 and 1996.)

My dream is that after reading this book, other entrepreneurs and business and industry executives, whose challenges and successes far exceed those of the BIC Alliance, will step forward to allow us the privilege of publishing books about their companies or their personal memoirs. I would love to publish a library of books on business and industry heroes and devote a portion of the revenue to helping tomorrow's entrepreneurs and executives. With more than 60 percent of the experienced executives and operations personnel in the energy business expected to retire in the next five years, we're witnessing today's protégés becoming tomorrow's mentors. Here at the BIC Alliance, our top priorities are to keep our flagship publication as America's No. 1 multi-industry, multi-departmental energy publication and continue growing IVS as a leader in executive recruiting and mergers and acquisitions, but we're also very willing to help train and inform tomorrow's leaders.

Another dream I have is to one day unite with other business and industry executives across America and build an industry entrepreneurs' hall of fame on I-10 that could be visited by young and old, allowing them to learn about one of America's greatest freedoms — entrepreneurship. (I find it interesting and challenging that we have numerous sports and music halls of fame, yet no industry hall of fame.)

So, what's in store for the immediate future? Sharing God's message of love, peace and perseverance, not only through our publications, but also during keynote presentations and training seminars. I look forward to management and sales training activities and to more speaking engagements not only in industry, but also with associations, nonprofit groups, youth groups, churches and even prisons. I'd love to launch a support group akin to Alcoholics Anonymous, where we'd guide fallen entrepreneurs to recovery and future success.

On a family note, Bodi and I will continue to be primary caregivers for her parents, and will spend as much quality time with Dane and Thomas and our grandchildren, Hannah, Mary and Michael, as we can. (At the time of this publication, Dane and Thomas had just celebrated their 15th anniversary in Italy while the kids stayed with us in Baton Rouge.)

We'll continue to mix business and leisure in our travels as our adventures take us not only across the Gulf South, but across America and internationally as well. We will also donate more time to helping those less fortunate. God has given us more than we ever dreamed of and now we want to pass that along to those who wish to fulfill their dreams.

Now that Thomas has taken over the day-to-day operations of the BIC Alliance and IVS, Bodi and I have more time to spend with him and Dane and our grandchildren, Hannah, left, Michael, center, and Mary.

Like many readers of *BIC* and this book, Bodi and I begin each day with a prayer of thanksgiving for the blessings and peace God has given us. We are living proof that the game is not over until the last play. In spite of decades of adversity, including near-death experiences, business failures, betrayals, family turmoil and lost loved ones, our love for God, one another, our family and the family of mankind has grown stronger with each blow. We've gone from dire poverty to entrepreneurial prosperity and are constantly reminded that being poor can be forever, but being broke is only temporary. Riches far beyond financial success are there for the taking for those with a love of God and a willingness to give it their all for the causes in which they believe.

It has always been my belief that most people, whether in business, industry or any other aspect of life, respect others who are willing to go the extra mile. Having traveled hundreds of thousands of miles doing bonus distribution of our publications across America, we at the BIC Alliance know a thing or two about that. In the early days, I'd load up an old Suburban with more than 200,000 miles on it and personally distribute *BIC* to industrial plants and energy-related service companies from Southeast Texas to South Louisiana. We'd also stuff our suitcases and pay our overweight fees so we could carry our publications on airplanes to trade shows and conferences across America. Often we'd take shifts driving to places like Nashville, Orlando or San Antonio and do bonus distribution at host hotels in the wee hours of the morning before hitting the sack. Today, I do these types of things for the pure enjoyment of meeting new people, the exercise and the fact that it keeps me humble.

One distribution-related incident I'll never forget took place during a visit to the Country Club of Louisiana in Baton Rouge a few years ago. I was carrying a stack of *BIC*s into the clubhouse when a banker to whom I'd turned for a car loan in the mid-'80s walked past me with a group of his friends. He greeted me with a sarcastic smile and said, "Hello Earl, I see you're still a paperboy!" His friends laughed. I smiled back and replied that the

One of my boyhood dreams was to some-day own a fleet of white Lincolns as a calling card for the successful company I'd one day own and manage. Shown here are "BIC 1" and "BIC 2", parked in front of our corporate office in Baton Rouge.

latest issue of *BIC* was hot off the press and I was anxious to share its good news. After dropping off the publications, I wished the men well and I returned to my new Lincoln with an inner smile that beamed.

You see, I was on my way to a home that I'd paid for in cash to change clothes for a weekend getaway to New Roads, where I planned to try out a boat I'd recently purchased. As I drove away, the sight of one of the banker's friends staring and pointing at my personalized license plate — which read "BIC 1"— was etched into my memory.

There was no need for me to respond to the banker in a rude way — I chose instead to let my success do the talking. Each day I meet hard-working folks who are teased by white collar individuals, many of whom are far less successful than those they are ridiculing. The point I'm making here is that you shouldn't judge a book by its cover. As my dad told me long ago, there are plenty of four-flush-ers out there who want you to think they have winning hands. He reminded me, however, that those who are holding the straight or royal flushes don't feel the need to brag or make fun of the cards others are holding because they're simply above that sort of behavior.

There was a time when I'd get irritated or feel sad when people would insult me or make light of how hard I worked, but that is no longer the case. Dad used to point his finger at me and say, "Son, God and Father Time will take care of you." He was right — God and Father Time have helped make me a better person through the many lessons they've taught me. Humility, inner strength and the importance of doing the right thing in every situation are just a few of those.

It is my hope that you will be similarly edified by this and the myriad other experiences about which you've just read. When life deals you a winning hand, instead of gloating, lay it down for others to see and humbly thank those who have helped you along the way. After all, it is nearly impossible to achieve victory in the game of life without first taking the hands of others who care about you and are willing to stand by you through thick and thin.

Now that you've read my story, I encourage you to begin writing your own, whether it's on paper or through your words and actions. God willing, this book will not only revive the weary, inspire those making fresh starts and uplift the broken hearted, but also motivate those with real ambition to pursue even greater heights. We also pray that all who read this book will

After we lost everything in 1982, it took 20 years of hard work, perseverance and the grace of God for Bodi and I to ultimately own the home of our dreams in Baton Rouge. It was in this peaceful setting that "It's What We Do Together That Counts" was written.

be blessed with a greater love of God, family and mankind.

Adversity or adventure. The choice is ours!

Part II:

Sources of Inspiration

Earl's Pearls of Wisdom

Regardless of your age, it is never too late to glean expertise, so long as you are willing to invest the time and energy necessary to achieve success.

(Below are selected passages from my writings in BIC and TLC, each of which will hopefully inspire you to seek greater peace, happiness and success in your business and/or personal life, whether you're looking for information on how to excel as a sales professional or how to develop a more positive outlook on life and all it has to offer.)

The Game of Life

I have always found one of life's great ironies to be that many of us seem more concerned with the performance and personal lives of professional athletes than we are with ourselves, our families, our friends and the companies with which we are associated.

You should realize that your life is the most important game you will ever play. If you do so, you will work to better condition yourself and your company.

Since this is a story about teamwork and the game of life, let's start with our own beginnings. Please join me in some creative thinking as we imagine the world we live in as a giant stadium in which the game of life is played daily.

When we are born, our parents and other family members are our coaches, spectators, greatest fans and, of course, our cheerleaders. We as young players make many mistakes. We stumble and fall, we take timeouts, and we are often penalized for our mistakes.

As we grow older, most of us learn the rules of the game of life and evolve into responsible athletes who become role models for our future generations.

In this game of life, we must play a wide variety of positions, some at different times, some simultaneously. Sometimes we're the rookie, sometimes we're the seasoned pro. We must be experts at both offense and defense.

We may even be the owner of the franchise, the manager, the recruiter, the coach or the assistant coach, but always, regardless of the positions, either on the field or throughout the stadium, there are two roles that each of us play that are ongoing.

We are both a player and a spectator.

Unfortunately, there are those of us who have become so out of shape mentally and physically that all we want to be is the complaining spectators — not willing to play the game ourselves, but finding no one who plays it well enough to suit us.

Even worse, some of us have become so complacent with our lot in life that we do not even bother going to the game, preferring merely to observe it from the comfort of our easy chair. Perhaps we have become so caught up in the beer and fast food commercials that our overindulgence has left us too exhausted to play any role except that of bystander.

It is important to remember that our minds must be exercised like our bodies, and that in order to maintain a winning edge, we must consistently learn.

The Importance of Continued Learning

In the business world, failure to grasp the intricacies of marketing and sales professionalism can mean the death of your opportunities for success, fame and fortune. It may cause you lifelong financial problems and the loss of respect from your family, friends and business associates. Worst of all, it may even result in a low sense of self worth.

The techniques and nuances of industrial marketing and sales are many and varied. Therefore, mastery of these arts do not come overnight. Rather, it is a process requiring a lifetime of learning. The manifold lessons involved are found not only in books and seminars, but are the result of extensive interaction with seasoned industry professionals who are willing to share their experiences. Regardless of your age, it is never too late to glean expertise, so long as you are willing to invest the time and energy necessary to achieve success.

I am a firm believer in the importance of continued learning. It has always been my belief that a salesperson should expand his or her knowledge beyond formal education and training, whether he or she is a beginner or a seasoned veteran.

Prospecting is the first step toward effective industrial marketing. I suggest that salespeople take what I call the "10 x 10 x 6" approach when developing a database of prospects. Using this approach, the salesperson should outline his or her top 10 prospects in 10 different industries, along with six contacts per company. In addition, using what I call the "3 x 3 x 3" approach, a salesperson should determine his or her three primary products or services, the three best reasons why another company should use those products or services, and the three best examples of a client using that product or service in a beneficial way.

With regard to making a sales presentation, communication is of paramount importance. I use the acronym "LISTEN" (look, interpret, stay alert, think, encourage and never interrupt) to illustrate how a typical sales call should be conducted.

Following are the key points of the LISTEN model:

Look: Always dress appropriately when calling on a potential client, but do not overdress. Do some research about the client before deciding what to wear.

Interpret: Use common sense to make the most of sales opportunities, and interpret what the company will be looking for and what will best help that company's bottom line.

Stay alert: Take notes, ask questions, give prospects choices and stay actively involved in the conversation.

Think: In discussing business with a potential client, the salesperson should possess the ability to think three-dimensionally, understanding the needs and objectives of both himself or herself and the buyer through third-person analysis. This allows the salesperson to better assess the situation, whether the buyer is eager or unwilling to make a deal.

Encourage: Encourage buyers to give more information about their companies. The more that is known about a company, the better the seller is able to establish a relationship and meet the needs of the customer.

Never interrupt: Interrupting is often a major mistake salespeople make when trying to push a sale. Instead, the salesperson should listen carefully to the concerns of the potential buyer and absorb the reasons why he or she is reluctant to accept a deal, if that is the case. The salesperson should then address the concerns one by one and counteract each reason with solid information designed to change his or her mind.

In order to effectively communicate benefits of a product or service, the salesperson should also know very well the product, the industry and the competition. Salespeople should also project what I call an "inner smile," an aura of positivity guaranteed to build the prospective buyer's trust in the seller's product or service and make a potential partnership more inviting.

Closing a deal is an end that is equally important to the means. When closing a deal, the salesperson should always establish with the buyer what the next step will be.

Networking is another important aspect of marketing a product or service. In order to successfully utilize the networking process, it is important to follow certain rules regarding who, what, when, where and how to network. (For example, the sales and/or marketing personnel should decide who the target audience should be, what is the desired effect of networking, when is the best time, where the best opportunities are available, and how the targeted audiences or companies can be reached.)

Networking is an integral part of life — both on the job and off. Your networking skills can bring you big business deals, great friends and fabulous places to vacation. You can read countless articles about networking techniques, but the most important thing you need to remember is to always treat others as you'd like to be treated. People never forget how you make them feel.

It's true that givers get. I try to build relationships by giving at least three good leads a day. I also make sure to say three nice things to people each day. People like to interact with folks who know how to listen, give referrals and say a kind word.

And, of course, when it comes to networking — practice, practice, practice. You know that you're doing a good job when someone comes up to you and says, "I've got someone I'd like you to meet." When someone introduces you to the most interesting person in the room — or your best prospect — that means you know what you're doing when it comes to networking. Here we see the law of reciprocity come into play — when you make others No. 1, they'll respond in kind.

Selling Our Ideas To Others

Success in our personal lives and business lives go hand in hand. Have you ever wanted something so badly that you blundered while trying sell your idea to the person or people who ultimately decided whether or not to help fulfill your desire and buy your product or idea?

First of all, it's important to remember that timing is everything. Even the best idea or product in the world can be rejected if it is presented at the wrong time. Recently my wife Bodi and I, along with our partners, Thomas and Dane Brinsko, planned to attend an LSU football game. We checked the weather report in the hours before kickoff — on that particular day, the likelihood of a thunderstorm was 90 percent. It was drizzling when we left our home.

Earlier in the day, knowing that the weather was going to be miserable, Thomas and I went to a store that sold LSU merchandise and stood in line with dozens of others who were buying rainwear. When the rains came during the game, we stayed dry while thousands of other spectators got drenched.

Timing and circumstances always play an important part in what, when and where we buy and must always be considered in what, when and where to sell.

We've always heard that the squeaky wheel always gets the grease. While we may think that our idea or product is the most important thing our bosses or our buyers should have on their "things to do list", the simple truth is that the priorities of others are rarely the same as our own. We've got to be able to put ourselves in the other person's shoes, whether you're a child dealing with a parent, a husband or wife selling an idea to a spouse, an employee selling an idea to a boss or owners or a salesman presenting a product or service to an existing client or prospect.

Here are a few ideas that you may want to think through very carefully when selling an idea, a product or a service.

— We never get a second chance to make a first impression.

— Manners matter in every presentation, especially in handling rejection. Losing our cool when we're rejected is the best way I know of to lose future opportunities to have our ideas and products selected. "No" doesn't necessarily mean "no" forever, it simply means "no" for now. So when we get a "no", we need to patiently try to find the best time and circumstances to present our idea or product again.

It's important that we know how to state our ideas clearly, whether they're spoken, written or expressed through other forms of non-verbal communication. It's also important to present the idea and proposal in such a manner that the person you're making your presentation to can easily explain to others your idea and/or product. So spend time preparing and practicing your presentation regardless of how large or small the opportunity might be. Building small relationships today can open big doors later and perhaps even bigger referrals immediately.

— Explain and show why your idea and/or product should be of value to the other person or organization.

— Share both the pros and the cons of the product or idea and address any objections as part of the presentation instead of waiting to hear them from the other person. It's been said that we should think of objections like weeds in a garden and pull them out regularly before they ruin the crops.

— Last but not least, offer several different options instead of seeking a yes- or-no response. I always approach a presentation as though I'm selling a Ford Motor Co. car or product. I offer the Lincoln, the Mercury and the Ford and explain that each option will get the driver where they want to go. The ultimate choice is just a matter of style, how they'd like to travel, the perception they'd like to create and the best investment at that particular time.

Compromise is the key component in selling an idea, whether it's at home or at work. If everyone isn't happy, no one is happy in the long run. Therefore, it is important to remember that our key long-term relationships are far more important than one-time sales. Furthermore, partial acceptance is better than no acceptance at all.

Controlling Anger

Over the years, I've had to end business relationships with people because of anger. Some have allowed their wrath to prompt them to resign. Others have had to be terminated because they couldn't get along with their colleagues.

Ending a hostile relationship with an angry person is like removing a cancer from the lives of both parties. It's the same way, perhaps even better, when we commit ourselves to removing anger from our own lives.

We must strive to live more harmoniously with others. We must practice patience and empathy. We must lead by example and train ourselves and those around us to do the same. When we make mistakes, we should apologize.

One of the best ways to prevent agitation from becoming anger is to confront the situation, discuss it with whomever you are having a problem and work together for a peaceful solution. Of course, the time to confront the situation is when emotions have subsided.

We can help make our relationships, our professions and our lives happier, healthier and more prosperous by thinking before we speak, speaking softly, taking the time to sleep on important decisions and remembering to confront negative situations at the right time in the right way.

Remember, people may forget what we said or did, but they will always remember how we made them feel.

The Importance of Laughter

One day while scanning a dictionary, I ran across the word

"laugh." I stopped to read more because just that morning, I was talking to my partner and son-in-law Thomas about the importance of enjoying life and the joy of laughter both at work and at home.

One of our main criteria at the BIC Alliance is not only to do a good job, but to have fun while doing it. There is no more uplifting feeling when I'm at work at my desk than to hear laughter among our staff members in another part of the building.

Laughter — that lyrical manifestation of unbridled joy — is one of the greatest gifts the Creator has bestowed upon us. Laughter makes the tedious less burdensome, the foreboding less gloomy and the distressing less worrisome.

I have known some folks who take life so seriously that I rarely, if ever, hear them laugh. Believe it or not, I know a few people whose only laughter is nothing more than an occasional smirk.

I can think of nothing sadder than encountering someone who does not know the utter exhilaration of simple, heartfelt laughter. Many people just don't know how to laugh. They never learned to laugh at life's little peccadilloes, at the sometimes dubious twists of fate, or perhaps most importantly, at themselves.

Some seem to laugh only for all the wrong reasons. How many people do you know who laugh only when being rude or condescending to others? How many find their amusement in the misfortunes of others?

I learned long ago not to take life too seriously, and that when it comes down to a choice between laughter or tears, laughter wins every time.

Making Work Fun

Making work fun is important — more so than many of us realize.

To most, having fun means laughter, liveliness, merriment and giving joy and pleasure to others. Of course, making money the old-fashioned way through honest, hard work can also be fun. Whether working in an industrial plant, on a drilling rig, at a construction site or in a corporate office, it can be immensely satisfying and enjoyable to deliver a quality product or service.

One of the best examples of a successful "fun" company is Southwest Airlines. Southwest has been selected No. 1 in the airline industry on many occasions and has been named one of the best companies to work for in America.

Southwest founder Herb Kelleher is one person who believes that work, business and fun should go hand in hand. If you believe in reading for fun and profit, I strongly recommend *Nuts!*, which is the amazing success story of Southwest Airlines. When I met Herb Kelleher in 1993, I was struck by how down-to-earth he was and how much fun he was to be around. Kelleher's *joie de vivre* carries over into the Southwest staff, making it one of the most enjoyable airlines on which to travel.

We have tried to instill the "work is fun" attitude at the BIC Alliance, both for our clients and staff members. We endeavor to make our marketing campaigns, trade show and conference participation, and other services as much fun as possible.

Making Your Job the Best Job

Enjoying your job is extremely important not only to your performance at work, but also to your entire approach to life. If you like your job, it can be the best job in the world.

What is the best job in the world? If we ask 100 people, we would surely get 100 different answers.

Surely clergymen feel they have the best job in the world, helping the members of their congregations in their search for salvation. Doctors, nurses, policemen and firefighters must feel the same about their professions — saving lives and helping prevent crime.

I believe that your attitude toward your job helps make it the best job in the world. If you find your work fulfilling, if you contribute not only to your livelihood, but to the good of others as well, what could be better?

You see, it's all a matter of perspective. The best job in the world means different things to different people, just as it means different things at different times to each of us. Too often we concentrate on the negative aspects of our jobs rather than accentuating the positive. However, I believe that even poor jobs can become better jobs with a positive attitude.

Unsung Heroes

The world is filled with heroes, but, if we were to rely solely on the news media, we might never know it.

Sometimes it seems that in this day and age, heroes are in short supply. All too often, the media are filled with words and images chronicling man's darker side, while the positive aspects, all the evidence of man's better nature, are for the most part ignored.

Of course, there are those exceptions when someone accomplishes some amazing feat. Two notable examples in recent years were former Sen. John Glenn's much-touted return to space at the age of 77 and former president George H.W. Bush's leap from an airplane in celebration of his birthday. But cases such as those of Glenn and Bush are rare, and those who attain that pinnacle of celebrity are indeed few and far between.

Then, too, there are those weekend warriors who have become heroes through their athletic prowess — the gridiron greats and diamond dazzlers who help propel their teams to victory as thousands of screaming fans cheer them on.

On occasion, there are those who achieve their 15 minutes of fame by reacting heroically in the face of tragedy. The attention of the nation is briefly focused on these individuals whose selfless actions have helped save the day.

But, for the most part, the modern-day hero goes steadfastly through life quietly and with dignity, seldom recognized, rarely heralded. These unsung heroes are the ones who help keep our world on track, the ones who are always there in the background ensuring the safe, sane continuity of our daily lives.

For each of us these champions may be different individuals, but each of them possesses the same strong vein of commitment, the same deep chord of dedication.

These unsung heroes are the teachers who give their all to our youth, helping mold young minds into the leaders of tomorrow. I remember three of my own elementary school teachers and the lasting impact they made on an impressionable young boy from Baton Rouge. Mrs. Gremillion, Mrs. Law and Mrs. Rae taught me not only an appreciation, but also a love for learning that I believe has served me well during the past half-century.

These unsung heroes are police officers, the men and women who put their lives on the line to protect ours. Seldom do these individuals receive even words of thanks, much less the recognition they deserve.

These unsung heroes are the firefighters who have dedicated their lives to saving people, homes and property. Often, these courageous souls never come to mind until we see their smoke-stained, battle-weary faces as our local news team covers the latest conflagration.

These unsung heroes are the men and women of the medical profession, the doctors and nurses and throngs of individuals who support their efforts.

These are the people who very often hold our very lives in their hands. Let us all be mindful of their deeds and afford them the gratitude they deserve when we encounter them. Also, each of us should strive to be unsung heroes not only for our children and grandchildren, but also for our co-workers and peers in industry.

Mentor-Protégé Relationships

A strong management team is crucial to success in any business. They must believe in the benefits of training, and they must be involved in those training efforts. They must also know that those new employees involved in the training program need to have a full understanding of every aspect of the business, and how every department and every function of the organization interrelates. Only when they realize how each member contributes to the team will they truly be one of its members.

As team leaders, we must do our part to make certain that everyone on our team is at the top of his game. We can accomplish this by sharing our own experiences so that they learn from the games we have played in the past. The same is true of leading by example. If we settle for mediocrity in an organization, that will never be a "championship" organization.

I sincerely believe that our leaders of tomorrow (our children, grandchildren and protégés) are anxious and excited to learn and use the knowledge they gain in their daily lives. I also feel that those of us who have accumulated that experience and knowledge should be just as excited to pass it on.

Our BIC Alliance team members who have been with us the longest seem to enjoy the mentor-protégé relationship. They take it upon themselves to help raise the level of everyone in our organization. They are quite often the ones who step forward and suggest ways we can serve our alliance members more efficiently and more effectively.

If your organization is lucky enough to include such individuals, it is your responsibility to encourage them and help them to grow every step of the way. Your business depends on it!

The Courtesy Phenomenon

Recently a young sales executive visited our Baton Rouge office for a crash course in strategic marketing and to cherrypick our databases for prospects.

Before leaving, the young lady asked me to share with her in a nutshell the keys to management and sales success. My responses were immediate — hard work, perseverance, learning, networking, asking questions and being courteous to everyone you meet, all the time. Courtesy, for instance, is one of the best investments that you can make in your business or personal life.

Stop and think about it for a minute — I'll bet that you can remember instantly not only the most courteous people you know, but also the companies whose employees treat you with the most courtesy.

Of all the compliments we receive here at the BIC Alliance, none is appreciated more or received more often than "Your folks are great to work with. They're all so nice, professional and courteous!"

In any organization, courtesy begins at the top and spreads like wildfire. The greatest manager I ever worked for was Merlin Keonecke, plant manager of Ethyl Corp., more than 30 years ago. Mr. Keonecke was one of the most soft-spoken, courteous men I've ever met. His skill was "management by walking around and asking questions." Every morning he would walk several miles, say hello to several hundred employees and stop in every plant to ask questions not only to managers, but also to craftsmen, operators and contractors. He would always begin with a courteous hello and ask how we were doing, how our families were doing, and how things were going in our units. Then he'd ask questions about specific things, i.e. rates, safety operations and maintenance problems.

When one of us couldn't answer a question that we were expected to know, Mr. Keonecke didn't raise his voice, criticize us or use profanity — his nonverbal cues were enough to let us know he was disappointed. Sometimes he'd say he was disappointed and that he expected us to have a better handle on things.

Once any of us experienced Mr. Keonecke's disappointment, we made it a point never to disappoint him again. By the time our plantwide meetings took place at 9 a.m., Mr. Keonecke had a better feel for the entire operation than every individual plant manager in the facility. And when we did something special he always made a point of recognizing us individually. He was loved by everyone, and our plant ran better under his watch than at any other time during my 15 years at Ethyl. I developed my management style more from Mr. Keonecke than anyone I know and am still trying to match his excellence after three decades.

It's important to note that being courteous involves more than good manners. It also includes mastering the art of listening, proper telephone etiquette and treating others the way you'd like to be treated. When Bodi and I stay at a hotel or eat at a restaurant, how the people treat us is more important than the quality of the room or the taste of the food.

Perhaps that's why we really enjoy working with people in the hospitality and travel industries — for the most part, they're more hospitable than people in other industries. In the energy business, most people are courteous, but some have a long way to go.

One interesting thing I've noticed is that folks who are "on the way up" in their professional lives are often less courteous than their supervisors and managers. Not long ago, I was planning to do a feature story about one of the South's top destinations for visitors. The person in charge of marketing and communications for that particular destination was so rude and condescending that we decided to feature an entirely different place.

Personally, I believe lack of courtesy has caused more people to lose promotions than lack of knowledge. In my own life, I know for a fact that I've accomplished more by being nice than I have by being smart.

So how do we change a lifetime of habits in one day? Start off one day at a time and try to be as courteous as you can each day. Try to say one nice thing to at least three people who deserve it each day, and observe their responses. Try saying "please" and "thanks" throughout the day, and "I'm sorry" when appropriate, and watch what happens. As you find life getting better and people enjoying your company more, you might even venture into uncharted territory like smiling regularly, letting folks out in traffic, returning phone calls, listening attentively or even sending a thank-you card or e-mail.

Once you've proved to yourself that this attitude is effective, try spreading courtesy throughout your company and your family. Just imagine a world where everyone, including our fellow citizens, spouses and children, were courteous to one another. You may be part of a new courtesy epidemic that spreads across America and around the world.

Well, it may take a while to spread around the entire world, but in a few weeks it can spread around the world in which most of us live.

But isn't that a great place to start?

A Story About Pride

In business and industry, when you're on the fast track, you are sometimes offered opportunities that cannot be refused without interrupting your momentum.

In the early '70s, an incident occurred at Ethyl Corp. that had such an impact on my life I'd be remiss if I didn't share it with you. Our company was doing a startup project in Israel, and it had sent several top superiors and foremen there to help manage it. One of our best leaders was a general foreman (I won't mention his name) who had been a role model for me, since we'd both been hired on as operators. He was so good at what he did that the idea of anyone being able to outperform him was simply beyond his comprehension.

This person had completed a year-long assignment, but then requested to come home. I, of all people, was selected to be his replacement, but the thought of spending six months to a year in a country far away from my wife and young daughter was like the assignment from hell to me. But how could I refuse without jeopardizing my career? Bodi and I prayed for an answer, and we soon received it.

I knew not only that we were having tremendous startup problems at the project, but also that I was expected to replace someone whose technical experience was broader than mine and that I'd need the help of our folks in the United States. However, I also felt that the prospect of replacing a person who viewed any potential replacement as being less competent might just work to my advantage.

We set up a conference call with our top management and technical folks and met at our main office in Baton Rouge in the middle of the night. When the general foreman and I got on the phone, we asked him to put together a list of all the problems he was facing so that I could consult with our experts about solutions before heading to Israel. I also asked for information about the strengths and weaknesses of co-workers so that we could defuse any potential personnel problems.

Less than 24 hours after our conference call, the person I was scheduled to replace made a decision that if he could get two weeks to visit the U.S., he'd prefer to return to Israel to see the project through.

The company was delighted, and my family and I were absolutely thrilled. While he was in Israel I continued to rise within the organization — I became a training coordinator, got a straight-day assignment and launched a side business that later became the BIC Alliance.

The moral of this story is that while pride can sometimes help you, other times it can be a hindrance. Every person has an Achilles' heel, but we shouldn't let pride or ego get us into adverse situations.

When Moby Dick Was a Minnow

There are many people who, when they reach a certain level in their careers, are so consumed with self-importance that they forget they reached that position by climbing the stairway to success one step at a time, not by suddenly appearing there as if by magic.

This scenario is perfectly summed up by a comment I once heard my good friend and longtime business associate Bud Howard of Volvo make when referring to a mutual acquaintance. Bud said, "I've known him since Moby Dick was a minnow."

Unfortunately, there are many folks with whom we come in contact that, while they may now have a whale of a title have somehow forgotten that they started out as just another minnow in a very big pond, struggling day to day to succeed.

These are the folks who are too busy to return phone calls because their time is much more valuable than anyone else's. They are the ones who constantly scan the crowded room or look over the shoulder of whomever they're speaking with to see if there is some-one else present who is more important.

One of my greatest pleasures in being a Moby Dick in industri-al marketing is always being able to recall my days as a minnow, and the favorable impression I had of those in higher places who treat-ed not only me, but each of us minnows as the most important per-son they knew.

These are the people who encourage others, the ones who make that climb up those stairs a bit easier. It is these people who should be recognized for the role they play in helping us grow from min-nows to leviathans.

The Secrets to Understanding People

How many books do you suppose have been written about improving people skills? Surely we could fill an entire room in our homes with all the words of wisdom that have been written about understanding people's needs.

Having trained adults and children for more than 40 years, I am constantly looking for new techniques and programs that help peo-ple to understand one another better, leading to happier and more meaningful and productive lives. Although there is no real "people encyclopedia" or even a small dictionary to which we can refer in order to learn the techniques we need most in dealing effectively with people, there are two secrets I've used successfully over the years that I'd encourage anyone to learn and practice.

The first secret I'm about to share — which was first brought to my attention when I read Les Gelpin's book, *People Smart* — has been field tested under the most adverse circumstances. Perhaps many of you have already mastered it. To my knowledge, there is no better secret to having a happier, more productive life. Most of us probably agree that in order to enjoy life to the fullest, it is important that we get along with others, that we know what makes people tick, what turns them on, and how human nature works.

The secret is to never threaten another person's survival. Imagine that you're in a building that has suddenly gone up in flames. There is only one exit, and everyone, yourself included, is crowding the door for escape, but there is only enough time for one person to make it through. Who would you want that person to be? Yourself, obviously, but that puts you in the same boat with everyone else. After all, survival is a human being's deepest psychological need.

No one likes to be crowded in a burning building or in their business or personal life. However, when you help someone else survive, they will appreciate you more.

Secret number two, also taken from *People Smart*, is that when you focus on others instead of yourself, they will respond in kind. This practice works every time and can change your life overnight. And it doesn't take millions of dollars in training or a Ph.D. in psychology to master — it just takes practice.

If you take the effort to practice the secrets mentioned above, you'll never forget the difference it will make in the way people will respond to you. Remember that no matter how much knowledge you have, people secrets are of little value unless you use them.

Making the Most of Life

It's been said that in our lives, each of us touches approximately 200 people. Just imagine if the 80,000 people who read each issue of *BIC* could bring a little greater happiness and a greater love for mankind to 200 people each. That's 16 million people — quite a lot of folks.

Let's be even more imaginative. Suppose those 16 million people could bring more love and happiness to 100 people each. That's

1.6 billion people. Wouldn't that be wonderful?

A few years ago, I saw on the news that television magnate Ted Turner would donate more than $1 billion over the next 10 years to causes in which he believed.

Whether or not we like Ted Turner, we cannot help but admire him for his actions. Not only is he dedicating his time and his personal resources, he is encouraging other wealthy people, in fact all of mankind, to do whatever is in their power to promote charity.

I did a great deal of soul searching in the weeks following my 1997 carjacking to determine how we at the BIC Alliance could do all in our power to help others not only become more productive, but also more community-conscious and family-oriented and to have a greater appreciation for life.

Even life's saddest, most challenging or most terrifying experiences can help us develop a happier, safer, more meaningful life if we can put them in perspective and gain some meaning from them.

One of the most meaningful aspects we can derive from these unpleasant experiences is keeping them in mind and passing the word along so that others are prepared when they face similar situations. Remember, from experience comes wisdom — we won't get burned ourselves if we listen to and heed the words of wisdom from those who have been burned before us.

Knocking On Doors

My favorite chapter in the Bible is Matthew, Chapter 7, particularly verses 1 and 6. In verse 1, Jesus tells us not to judge or we too will be judged. For in the same way we judge others, we will be judged and with the same measure we use to mete out judgment to others.

"Why do you look at the speck of sawdust in your brother's eye and pay no attention to the plank in your own eye?" Jesus continues.

In verse 6, Jesus says, "Do not give dogs what is sacred; do not throw your pearls to pigs. If you do, they may trample them under foot and then turn and tear you to pieces."

Verses 7 and 8, however, are verses that I recommend to every person seeking peace, happiness and success in their spiritual, business and personal lives — "Ask and it will be given you, seek and you will find, knock and the door will be opened to you. For everyone who asks receives, he who seeks finds and to those who knock, the door will be answered."

My interpretation of these two verses is this: Ask for God's forgiveness and love, and you will receive it. Ask for and seek peace, happiness and success, and they will be yours. And, knock on doors. To me, knocking on doors means not only to go to work, but also to work hard and be persistent.

My life provides an example of how putting God first leads to more personal peace, happiness and financial success than you can even dream of. However, we can't just ask for great things to happen. We've got to knock on doors and share the good news with others. Try it and see what happens — I think you will be astonished just like I've been.

An Affirmation

More than a decade ago I drafted a New Year's resolution by which I have come to try and live my life and manage the BIC Alliance. I feel that it offers a clear view of what's in store for the future of our family and the BIC Alliance.

It goes like this:

"As we prepare for the new year, I will do my best to be a good Christian, a good husband, a good father and grandfather, a good friend and a good business associate. At the BIC Alliance, we will keep our spirits high and we will endeavor to bring happiness and business success to those whom we serve.

We will work hard for our BIC Alliance members and readers and make as many referrals as possible to help them generate new business and fulfill their needs.

We shall work diligently to create safe, clean and profitable workplaces across America and the world. We shall work to protect the environment and to help those less fortunate than ourselves.

We shall conduct ourselves in a manner that is a tribute to our family, our friends, our colleagues, our clients and our country. We shall never treat anyone in a condescending manner, and we will do our best to eliminate prejudices and negative attitudes.

Our door will always be open for those in need of someone with whom to talk and/or share ideas, suggestions and opinions. Regardless of how busy we are, we shall always try to spend quality time with our families and friends.

The business and community service objectives of our BIC Alliance members will become our own. We will work each day to make our community and country a safer and better place to live."

I encourage you to draft similar resolutions on paper and reaffirm them on a yearly basis. After all, people are significantly more likely to meet objectives that are written rather than trusted to memory.

100 Tips for Achieving Peace, Happiness and Success

1) Make God, family, friendship and kindness to others your top priorities.

2) Say one nice thing to at least three people each day.

3) Join and become active in the organizations related to your profession.

4) Focus on being more interested instead of being more interesting.

5) Treat others as you would like to be treated instead of treating them the way they treat you.

6) Stay away from anything that can become a dangerous addiction.

7) Learn and practice the art of listening.

8) Attend church regularly and take notes. Taking notes helps trigger memory.

9) Don't be afraid to share God's good news with others.

10) Make wholesome leisure activities part of your life.

11) More people become successful because they're nice than because they're brilliant.

12) First impressions are important — we never get a second chance to make one.

13) Keep good business and personal financial records.

14) Share your wealth with others, beginning with your church.

15) Save regularly. It's not how much you earn, it's how much you've got when you need it that counts.

16) Learn and practice the art of networking by making three excellent referrals per day.

17) Keep a business journal and a family journal and review them regularly.

18) When mistakes happen, learn from them.

19) When you've wronged someone, apologize and ensure it does-

n't happen again.

20) Don't be afraid of hard work. It won't kill you.

21) Set written business and personal goals — daily, weekly, monthly and annually.

22) If you supervise others, know and review their goals at least monthly.

23) Get involved in your community's activities.

24) Practice what you preach. No one likes a hypocrite.

25) Practice safety and environmental consciousness on the job and off.

26) Become a positive role model at work and at home.

27) Before speaking, think about how the person listening will interpret what you say.

28) Encourage others instead of putting them down.

29) Read the Bible regularly. Highlight important verses.

30) Never stop learning. The more we learn, the more we earn.

31) Remember that you can control and change the things you think about.

32) Don't discriminate toward others on the basis of race, color, religion or economic status.

33) Seek mentors for yourself and become a mentor to others.

34) Listen to motivational speakers, tapes, preachers, etc.

35) Spend time thinking. Learn how to harness the power of thinking for productive means.

36) Learn and practice effective time management techniques.

37) Learn how to dress and dine properly (I learned these and other helpful tips on professional etiquette from longtime BIC partner and friend Dr. Shirley White of Success Images).

38) Practice courtesy to others. People never forget how we make them feel.

39) Learn and practice good verbal communication skills.

40) Thank people regularly for their business, help, etc.

41) Surround yourself with honest, ethical, hard working people.

42) Stay away from negative people, places and situations.

43) Be kind to the elderly. Remember, you're going to be elderly yourself one day.

44) Devote special time for loved ones, family and friends.

45) Before you evaluate others, ask them to evaluate their own performance.

46) Refrain from profanity. It's unpleasant and makes you look bad.

47) It's just as easy to wear a smile as a frown.

48) Don't pout or carry grudges. If God can forgive us, we should be able to forgive one another.

49) Build a library of motivational/how-to books and magazines and read them.

50) Pray regularly and give thanks for your blessings instead of praying only in times of trouble and/or despair or when you want something.

51) If you're in management or sales, strive for professionalism. In America, only one in 10 salespeople are true professionals. That means that only about 1.3 million out of 13 million salespeople are professionals.

52) Practice self control in all that you say and do.

53) Know what to do in emergencies (fire, accident, heart attack, family crisis, etc.).

54) Remember that not everything that glistens is gold.

55) Document fond memories and experiences in pictures, video, audio tapes, etc.

56) Practice presentations before making them. A great way to do this is to videotape yourself making a presentation or watch yourself in a mirror acting as both the buyer and the seller.

57) When speaking or making a presentation, be prepared for any-

thing or any question that might arise.

58) No one's perfect, but that shouldn't stop you from striving for perfection.

59) Believe, and you will receive.

60) We can fool some of the people some of the time, but not all of the people all of the time.

61) In the land of the lazy, a hard worker with vision knows no limits.

62) Research and prospecting are the keys to successful entrepreneurship and sales. It's not "see more and you'll sell more" — it's more about prospecting better and then seeing more of the best prospects.

63) Early to bed and early to rise makes a person healthy, wealthy and wise.

64) Remember what it was like at the bottom, and help others reach the next rung on the ladder of success.

65) It is more blessed to give than to receive.

66) Find a great partner. God only knows where I'd be without my wonderful wife and soulmate, Bodi.

67) Remember, Abe Lincoln lost many times before becoming a winner. Never give up!

68) Be proud to be an American. Show your pride by voting.

69) Stop complaining. Nobody likes to be around a whiner.

70) Watch peoples' faces when you enter a room. Do they smile or frown?

71) Learn to master non-verbal communication to influence others — facial expressions, tone of voice, listening, etc. Since 90 percent of our communication is non-verbal, it's important to remember that actions speak louder than words.

72) When making presentations one-on-one, use a pen to diagram and explain things better. This also helps maintain attention.

73) Preview before you begin a meeting, and review after you finish a meeting.

74) It's just as easy to sell a Rolls Royce as it is a Chevrolet. You just don't have to sell as many of them!

75) Always remember that there are two sides to every story.

76) Love and forgiveness go hand in hand. It's hard to have one without the other.

77) One of the great things about starting at the bottom is that there is plenty of room to advance.

78) When we point a finger at someone, there are always three pointing back at us.

79) It's better to be perceived as a fool than to open your mouth and leave no doubt.

80) The best form of self-evaluation is to ask yourself, is God proud of me? Setting out to make Him proud every day is a great goal.

81) Visualizing where you want to be is the first step on the journey to success.

82) There is no big "I" or little "U" in team.

83) Give praise in public. Criticism, however, should be done in private, even when it's constructive in nature.

84) Compromise is better than confrontation. Find the middle ground where everyone is comfortable.

85) Learn and respect the different personality types and communicate with others based upon theirs, not on your own.

86) Knowing how to utilize space and tone of voice are the cornerstones of effective communications and sales. These techniques are easily learned and should be practiced daily.

87) Alligators don't have vocal cords and strike only when the time is right. Emulate these creatures by listening and learning before taking action.

88) Don't let the devil keep bringing up the past. God gives us a

new start every day.

89) True success comes when we've reached the point where we are more concerned with doing what's right than obtaining money, publicity and/or recognition.

90) Just because we graduated at the top of our class in the school of hard knocks doesn't mean we can't earn a doctorate in success.

91) Show me a person who is afraid to lose his or her job, and I'll show you a person who most likely will.

92) Selling is more fun and profitable when we sincerely believe that our product or service is to our prospective buyers what spinach is to Popeye.

93) If you're writing a book, keep in mind the following tip from Ben Franklin: write things worth reading and do things worth writing about.

94) Before we can manage others effectively, we must master self-management.

95) Always remember to laugh with others, not at them.

96) A smiling face is the best way I know of to end a conversation or a personal note.

97) The best way to build self-confidence is to know how to act properly and say the right things at the right time.

98) Attitude is more important than aptitude in determining altitude.

99) Make adversity an adventure by finding the rainbow in the storm.

100) Remember — it's what we do together that counts!

Success Secrets From the Experts

(On the following pages, you'll find insights into success both inside and outside the workplace given by successful executives and entrepreneurs representing different businesses and sectors of industry, many of which have been pulled from the pages of BIC and TLC.)

"When I began industrial work as a frightened 20-year-old boy, I had a lot to learn. I was awed and astounded by the multitude of details that I had to learn. One night, an older operator gave me some advice that has shaped my life all these years. He said, 'Son, don't worry about all you have to learn — just learn one new thing every day.' I took his advice. Consequently, the more I learned, the more I wanted to know. It is true that knowledge is power. This made me ambitious in a healthy way. It also carried over into my spiritual life and brought a closer walk with God. It wasn't long before promotions began to come.

Soon, I was working above my education level and enjoying it. My future seemed to be established. I figured I would retire as a millionaire. Then, my life took a drastic turn. The lord called me to pastor full-time. This meant giving up the job that I loved with all my heart and going away to school. Then, I loved school so much that I could have become a professional student. However, my money was gone, and my family needed attention. I stopped the educational process with a doctorate in ministry. I have been privileged to pastor eight churches. Seven out of the eight churches experienced great growth. I cannot, and will not, try to take the credit for what God has done.

Now, I am facing another crisis in my life. I am 68 years old with declining health. I now realize my days as a full-time pastor are numbered. However, the same drive and ambition that began with learning is still in me. I am resolved not to become a couch potato. I am considering some things that I want to write about. While I try my hand at writing, I will also do pulpit supply and interim work. While there are lots of things I would like to say to the young generation, there is one thing I must say. Knowledge is power! Learn one new thing every day!" — **Dr. Gerald Hull, pastor of Burning Bush Baptist Church in Walker, La., 2005 —**

"It runs against common thought, but helping others is the path to success in life. If by faith we are taught 'Love others as you love yourself,' then surely within that concept we are called to help one another. Help is one of the most visible and tangible aspects of the selflessness that love requires. That helping/loving others will lead to success is true in every aspect of life, whether it be parental, marital, social, managerial or servile.

I'd like to share two specific work-related examples of how helping others will put you squarely on the path to business success. The first is to find and develop a relationship with a mentor. Choose him or her carefully, and then be willing to do all of the work delegated to you. In exchange, you will learn your trade correctly, and, additionally, when your mentor climbs the ladder of success based in part on your work, he or she will pull you up the ladder behind them.

The second is to join relevant professional associations and participate through contribution of effort. In exchange for the effort put into work on committees and/or the boards of professional associations, you will learn more about the industry as a whole and broaden your network of meaningful contacts.

Like much wisdom, it seems quite self-evident when you hear it or read it. These two specific tips were shared with me by Earl Heard before I started my first day on the job with Exxon. At the time, it didn't surprise me that both tips were related to hard work and learning, but it didn't occur to me until much later that they had a deeper commonality; they both required working for the benefit of someone or something else. Serving others humbly will increase your individual status. They are practical applications of the ancient and biblical principles, 'Love others as you love yourself,' because 'It is better to give than to receive.' Or, as Earl might say, 'It's what we do together that counts.'" — **Thomas Brinsko, president and chief operating officer of the BIC Alliance and Ind-Viro Search, 2005 —**

"The servant leader is the steward of the culture of the organization. Servant leadership is driven by the cumulative words, thoughtful acts of service, praise, correction and coaching of the CEO and his subordinates. Great corporate cultures improve the character of every team member." — **John Lake, CEO of Rain for Rent, 2005 —**

"In some ways, starting a business is like cooking a good jambalaya. You must have all the right ingredients, or it will not turn out right.

You need good partners, loyal employees and customers, honesty, integrity, loyal and fair investors, sufficient capital, a good banker and lawyer(s), competitive insurance agents, a great product line, a good advertising method, a good plan and budget, plenty of determination, and the willingness to take the risks you will face." — **David Starkey, president and CEO of Empire Scaffold, 2005—**

"I have lived by a simple rule of management both in my business life and my personal life. As a person advances in his or her career, be sure to treat that person like you want to be treated because you will likely meet the same people as your career winds down. Therefore, make sure your reputation remains true to your character in business and your family life." — **Kent Wasmuth,**

area director of sales and marketing for the Wyndham New Orleans Hotel at Canal Place, 2005 —

"A very successful businessman turned my life around more than 10 years ago when he spoke to over 2,000 business men and women at a meeting in Atlanta and said to all of us: 'Whether you believe me or not, I know that if you aren't putting God first in your life, you'll never truly be successful in any job or business!'

That day, I gave my life to God and found the true key to happiness and success was having the proper alignment or priorities in the correct order: God, family, job/business. With God as my pilot, my personal and professional life has been blessed abundantly. Furthermore, all of us meet obstacles in our life, but it is, in my opinion, the entrepreneurial spirit that allows us to look beyond the obstacles and challenges and become overcomers in life." — **Margie Larson, retirement community marketing director, 2005 —**

"It is my judgment that there are two keys to success. First is self-confidence, and second is self-discipline. The best way to gain more self-confidence is through education. Education is a lifelong process, just as success is achieved over a lifetime. You must believe you can be successful, and education will show you the way. Self-discipline is about choices. Your parents can discipline you for a few years, but it is up to you to make choices that will make you and your parents proud. The bottom line is, I hope self-confidence and self-discipline will serve you to the utmost based on your ability and desire to succeed in this world of dreams." — **Leon J. Kinchen, president of Bottomline Money Management, Inc., 2005 —**

"I am a firm believer in training and self improvement through reading and educational seminars. I believe that leadership and management are learned skills. Additionally, we at Baker Tanks take pride in developing a culture that I make certain we reinforce with Baker people redundantly. We will do the right things based

on customer expectations, with our individual actions strongly entrenched in the highest standards of ethics and integrity that ensure that the Golden Rule has formed our foundation for customer service and communication. The point is, customers trust that we will say what we will do, and that we will do what we say."
— Bill St. Amant, division vice president of Baker Tanks, 2005 —

"The reason that I feel successful is because I am getting paid to do what I absolutely love doing. My advice to young people who are looking for success is to ask themselves, 'What am I good at? What do I really enjoy doing?' Once you figure that out and can identify realistic pursuits, go for it!

Get the necessary education. Education doesn't always come wrapped up in a university classroom. Try getting different jobs in your interest areas. Don't lose sight of reality — there aren't a lot of openings for astronauts or even marine biologists. But someone managed to become those, so why not you? If you are happy and proud of doing what you do, you will throw yourself into your work with greater zeal than someone else who isn't as fulfilled. It only stands to reason that you will then have more success. If you are good at doing something that you don't enjoy, you can't really consider yourself successful by my definition. Life is too short to spend such a large share of your life doing what might pay you good money but give you no joy for your efforts. Life might be a box of chocolates according to Forrest Gump, but the people who have excelled at what they do in their lives and are fulfilled and proud — they are eating the Godivas." **— Walt Lehmann, global marketing director of Celanese PBI, 2005 —**

"Forty years ago, as I was starting my professional life, a friend and colleague gave me the following advice: 'Happiness is about interpersonal relationships.'

More and more every day, I realize how right he was. As I

reflect on both my personal and professional life, I realize that it is people who make the difference. My wife, my children, my colleagues, my customers and others in the community are what have brought happiness and success. If you find a vocation/profession that you are passionate about, then going to work is both rewarding and fun. If you give back to your community, then you make a difference in others' lives, and nothing is more gratifying. I have been fortunate to experience business success, and I am very pleased about that. But, most of all, I am proud of the relationships I have had with my family, my teammates and all the people I have met along the way. If you are passionate about what you do, never compromise your ethics and value others, then success will inevitably follow." — **William S. "Bill" Slaughter, Ph.D., president of SSA Consultants, 2005 —**

"Anyone can realize their dreams through hard work, perseverance, kindness and respect for others. My theme in life is that you must first dream and then enjoy life while fulfilling your dream(s). Life is too short to stress over things you have no control over or being in relationships, situations, etc., that are not fulfilling and do not impact your life in a positive way. So, I say, have some values (treat people like you would have them treat you), respect yourself and others, dream big and live life to its fullest. And, last, but not least, continuously give thanks to God for everything!" — **Debra G. Robinson, marketing representative for PBI Performance Products, Inc., 2005 —**

"I do not think you can compartmentalize happiness, peace and success within the various segments of your life — family, friends, work, etc. Realization of these goals will only happen when God's proper balance is recognized and achieved. He wants you to work hard and be interested in your career and add value to your employer, employees and customers, and accumulate wealth. He may want

144

you to have a family, to love them, provide for them, protect them and spend time with them. He wants you to have friends, spend time with them and enjoy their company. He wants you to have other interests, enjoy your free time and play hard. But success as the world sees it and sells it places the emphases and priorities in the wrong order, never resulting in true success. That will only occur when we make our relationship and fellowship with God our first priority. This will always be a work in progress, as we are continually seeking His will for our lives, working to be obedient, living for others and putting ourselves last. This is a constant struggle for most of us, because it is not our nature, and most of the forces around us support the opposite. But, when we do this, all the other aspects of our lives will go much better, and we can feel and work toward the 'success' we are all seeking." — **Don Fanning, vice president of marketing and contract administration for Austin Industrial, 2005 —**

"Curiosity is the key to happiness for me in my business and personal life. Wondering about how something works or how it might work better sparks creativity. Wanting to see what something really looks like, sounds like or even smells like results in travel, study and great conversations. Another important factor in my life that keeps me moving and doing (which is when I am the happiest) is the realization that there is no going back; this is it, and you are doing what you always wanted to do right now! The kids will never be like they are right now — enjoy them. If you can buy that ranch you always wanted, do it now — there is no better time. If you want to see the national parks, set up an agenda right now and go see one.

Two of my greatest annual exercises are 1) listing all the gigantic and small things I want to do in my lifetime, and 2) listing all of the "tolerances" I am allowing to drain my energy. Tolerances are big and small things that you do not like, but put up with for whatever reason; tolerances are constant, usually low-level irritants that dampen happiness. Once these lists are made, magic happens. The lifelong dreams become reality, and the tolerances just get handled!

So, my advice on being happy is to be curious, remind yourself of your dreams and truly live the moment." — **Helen I. Hodges, president of Separation Systems Consultants, Inc., 2005 —**

"In my business, I know for a fact that many of my customers could probably find as good a product or service somewhere else, but most do not. I attribute this mainly to the utmost and sincere courtesy that I try to extend to every single customer I serve, large and small." — **Kevin Browning, sales manager for KeepSafe Inc., 2005 —**

"On May 1, 1987, I left the security of a large accounting firm to start my own CPA firm. Many of my peers thought I was crazy, while many of my friends were cautiously optimistic. I was 29 years old, with seven years of experience. The local economy was down, but my confidence was up. I had recently completed a Dale Carnegie course on human relations and a light had come on in my head — I could do it, I could start my own business. I had the technical knowledge, determination and organizational skills; all I needed was a business plan and a lot of help.

First, I had to help myself. For months, I did my homework and prepared a solid business plan. I did not dwell on the negative, even when a close friend/banker scoffed at my idea. I stayed positive and another banker believed in me and loaned me the start-up funds (of course I had to risk $8,000 of my own money). The business plan included a 'worst-case scenario' game plan, which negated any anxiety. Another advisor/friend suggested I lease an office in a high-traffic location where I could get free exposure. He also told me, 'Keep your head down and work hard.' This was simple, but sound advice. In other words, the first lesson was, 'Success starts with you.'

The next lesson I learned was to ask successful people for help. I asked experts I knew to help me set up computers, find employees and assist me in networking to find clients. And to my surprise, it all worked out. That was 18 years ago and the firm has grown almost every year. I can't begin to thank all the great people who have helped me.

Looking back, I realize that I wanted to experience the challenge of running my own business and being financially successful, but I also wanted to have fun. I wanted to enjoy work! I really enjoy making clients laugh or smile first before we get down to business (IRS agents are a bigger challenge). My firm's goal is to solve clients' financial and tax problems and send them home happy — there is just no other way to do business. We cannot have any unhappy clients.

I also enjoy a balance of work and personal life. Starting out, I found company outings and 'business-after-hours' activities offer good opportunities to blend work and leisure. Later, I found family time to be a higher priority. Overtime has always been flexible and never excessive, even during tax season. 'Rest before you get tired,' is a good motto to avoid burnout. Once, as a young accountant, I asked my boss if I should come in on Saturday to finish a project. He looked at me with an ironic smile and said 'No, work is going to be here long after you and I are gone.' Amen to that." **— Michael Choate, president of Michael Choate and Co., CPAs, 2005 —**

"When I take credit for my accomplishments, I am soon to fail. When I give God credit, I cannot fail." **— Joel Campanile, owner of Ascension Marine, 2005 —**

"In today's rapidly changing world, a successful manager must possess superior people skills and an endless desire to learn. Quality and satisfaction are no longer just desirable, but rather must be deeply imbedded in the company's core values and its objectives and goals. To meet and exceed customers' expectations will guarantee a company's long-time success and financial health. The willingness and the ability to share the company's success with as many people as possible makes one's professional life more interesting, rewarding and worthwhile." **— Hans U. Wandfluh, president and general manager of the Royal Sonesta Hotel in New Orleans, 2005 —**

"Work hard, get a mortgage and remember to be nice to everyone. Today's office boy will be tomorrow's client!" **— Peter A. Mayer, chairman of the board of Peter Mayer Advertising, 2005 —**

"Henry David Thoreau said, 'If one advances confidently in the direction of his dreams, and endeavors to live the life which he has imagined, he will meet with success unexpected in common hours.'" **— Clifford E. McFarland, president of McFarland, Grossman & Co., Inc., 2005 —**

"I think that, all too often, young people think they are limited in certain ways. There are a lot of people who say 'I could've done that, or I should've done that,' but there are very few who actually step up and try. Sometimes trying involves risking your reputation and/or your financial well-being. It's OK to fail in the beginning. We've seen a lot of people fail. I think that Presidents Reagan, Bush and Clinton all lost elections at one time or another. They saw failure firsthand. Also, I believe it was Abraham Lincoln who said that great things come to those who wait, but better things come to those who hustle." **— Jim Bernhard, CEO and founder of The Shaw Group, Inc., 2005 —**

"You have to stay optimistic. If you don't, who is going to? Someone has to keep focused on the future and say, 'Yes, we have issues now, but we are going to get through them one bite at a time, and we are going to emerge as the best.' Because if you don't believe it as the manager, who is going to believe it?" — **Lori Ryerkerk, refinery manager of the ExxonMobil Beaumont, Texas, refinery, 2005 —**

"In my mind, the keys to my success have been belief in myself and belief in others. There are many who train and speak who have a 'story' to tell — I simply don't. My inspiration comes from the fact that I had a great family — we weren't rich, but I certainly didn't grow up in poverty. Neither of my parents finished college, but they both worked. The environment in which I was raised was one of optimism. Something that my mother and father always encouraged me to do was to try my best and shoot for the stars. Something I have found that's an absolute insight I have gained is to try to surround yourself with positive people. Everybody needs somebody. We can't do this all by ourselves. I've had a lot of friends and clients who have rooted for me in my successes and cried for me in my failures.

I've always been a dreamer. Yet, you have to have an action plan and follow through. My favorite saying is 'Keep on keepin' on!'" — **Dr. Shirley White, president of Success Images, 2005 —**

"Creating an effective team is one of the most dynamic and exciting things about any of our human interactions, especially in the business world. In a lot of traditional businesses, people are divided, but you can accomplish more if you come together and capitalize on one another's strengths and work together to overcome one another's weaknesses." — **Paul Mott, president of the New Orleans Hornets, 2005 —**

"God is not intimidated, worried or weak-kneed about a problem. I know He could make it go away, but generally does not. I do know that He is going to walk me through it. He is always there and will always provide guidance if you listen." — **Mark Albers, president of ExxonMobil Development, 2005 —**

"My philosophy is to be honest, expect a lot from your people and create an atmosphere where hard work becomes fun." — **Frank Marine, vice president of environmental sales and marketing for Texas Molecular, 2005 —**

"I think there are a lot of ways to define success beyond position or status. My faith-based Christian perspective has guided me throughout my life. I continue to remind myself that we are all human beings, and we are all deficient in some fashion and need help. None of us has all the answers. The important thing is to cooperate with one another and listen to each other to understand how we might all be better collectively than we are individually." — **David M. Ratcliffe, chairman, president and CEO of Southern Co., 2005 —**

"You have to have an ability to work with people. That stems from being able to generate a vision that can be shared with a lot of folks and empowering them to reach that vision." — **Al Anderson, plant manager of Tesoro's Mandan, N.D., refinery, 2005 —**

"Leaders need to share the vision, inspire the people and hold them accountable to achieve." — **Doug Quinn, refinery manager for Motiva's Convent, La., Refinery, 2004 —**

"You have to be in communication with your team constantly, and that means listening as well as talking. Also, you have to have a sense of humor." — **Stephen Tisdale, president and general manager of Aluma Systems Concrete Construction Division, 2004 —**

"If you build a good team and take care of your people, the rest will fall into place. That philosophy will build a good business in any field." — **Alan Barnhart, president of Barnhart Crane and Rigging Co., 2004 —**

"If you see an opportunity to do something on your own, although it could be hard for a few years, I would always advise that you try it." — **Merv Litzow, president and founder of Safeguard Technology, 2004 —**

"Your ability to change faster than the competition may be your only real competitive advantage, but it is the people who really make a difference. Leaders must not forget this simple truth." — **Steve Rathweg, site manager for Shell Chemical in Geismar, La., 2004 —**

"There are things that have to be done right away, but there are also a lot of things that will influence your company's success that take a while to develop. You have to set your level of expectations properly, and then manage those expectations and, in many cases, that requires some practice." — **David LaCoste, vice president of the Gulf Coast region for Onyx Environmental Services, 2004 —**

"Keep your running shoes on. If you are sitting still, you are backing up, and the market will change right underneath you." — **Todd Foust, president and owner of Coating Services, Inc., 2004 —**

"I try to treat people in the same way that I would like to be treated. As you go through life and your career, the simple things sometimes make the difference." — **Harold Kergosien, president and COO of Buckeye Gulf Coast Pipe Lines, 2004 —**

"If you don't spend the time and money to develop strong employees, you aren't going to survive very long." — **Bill Myers, co-owner and vice president of Oilind Safety, 2004 —**

"Work, work, work, and the harder you work, the luckier you are. Know what is needed by your customers." — **Forrest Shook, founder and CEO of NLB Corp., 2004 —**

"You must have a vision and a philosophy. However, that is not enough. You must also have a strategy that operationalizes what you want to achieve. The most difficult lesson that I have learned in business is that you have to continuously improve every aspect of your business or you risk losing market share." — **Jack Pankoff,**

president, CEO and founder of TTS Performance Systems, Inc., 2004 —

"Business concepts and ideas should be constantly challenged in order to ultimately identify the best option. This practice also helps you to stay aligned with your people, keeping everyone on course and striving for the same goal." **— Bill Stoll, president of Praxair Services, Inc., 2004 —**

"If you don't follow up with your customers, they will go somewhere else." **— Brian Battle, co-owner of DeHumidification Technologies, 2004 —**

"Before you begin a project, you need to make a little extra research to avoid duplicating what others have done in that area." **— Dr. Michel Daumerie, vice president of research and technology for ATOFINA Petrochemicals, 2004 —**

"You have to have the courage to try things and keep what works. Without change, there's no improvement." **— Roger Gossett, president of Brock Specialty Services, 2004 —**

"Be decisive and deal with conflict head-on. Letting needed decisions linger creates confusion, causes a perceived sense of a lack in direction to your organization and fuels conflict. I have seen managers who believe conflict in an organization is healthy, but I just don't believe it. Conflict separates your team into individuals who aren't working together toward one common goal." **— Gary Gardner Jr., vice president and country manager of Furmanite America, 2004 —**

"If you listen, people will tell you what they want." **— Catherine Cloy, president and CEO of the Safety Council, 2004 —**

"Leadership is influence, nothing more, nothing less." **— Alan Thomas, vice president of the Safety Council, 2004 —**

"There's something about making a product each day, and then seeing it out in the marketplace that makes you feel like you've accomplished something." — **Bruce March, refinery manager for ExxonMobil Refining & Supply Co. in Baton Rouge, La., 2003 —**

"Never underestimate the need for capitalization in a developing company. It always takes longer and costs more to break even than you anticipate. Find strong financial partners who will help you get through the growing pains. If you have that, along with a real service or product or service providing measurable benefits to a large client population, you'll be unstoppable." — **Mike Scott, president and CEO of InTANK Services, 2003 —**

"There's no other way to be successful than to work as a team." — **Otis Hall, vice president and general manager of BASF in Geismar, La., 2003 —**

"Listen to your customers. Listen to other successful business owners. Listen to your conscience. Listen to your employees. Good, basic communication is not only good marketing, it's good business practice." — **Jim Robinson, Jerry Strickland and Mike Walton, founders of AltairStrickland, 2003 —**

"Listening to the people with whom you work is vital. They will help you understand the problems they face, and they will help you see things from a different point of view." — **Jeff Utley, senior vice president of operations and plant manager of Flying J, Inc. in North Salt Lake, Utah, 2003 —**

"You must learn your business from the ground up. You must be capable and willing to make sacrifices, but you have to start at the bottom in order to appreciate your employees' and your customers' perspectives." — **Keith Smith, president of American Industrial Craftsmen, 2003 —**

"You've got to have a sound financial structure going into business." — **Gerald Pruitt, owner and president of Bronco Construction, 2003 —**

"Surround yourself with the best talent available. Clearly define and communicate expectations, and measure performance against those expectations. Accept accountability for improvement. Encourage positive, proactive behaviors, and then let the people do their jobs." — **Jeff Davis, president of Brock Maintenance, Inc., 2003** —

"Success comes with a coherent vision and the capacity to implement it." — **Edward Gosselin, president and CEO of GOTAR Technologies, Inc., 2003** —

"It's important to assess people and their performance, and to counsel and teach people." — **Ray Commander, senior vice president of operations/plant manager for Intercontinental Terminals, 2003** —

"I work from a basic philosophy that success comes with pride. I believe you teach people to be successful and you empower them to make decisions. When you believe in your people and have confidence in them, they will grow your business and satisfy your clients." — **Jon Hodges, president and founder, Evergreen Environmental Services, 2003** —

"Once you have the right people, give them the right skills. Then make sure you are clear cut with goals and objectives and provide them the resources they need to achieve these goals." — **Dave Cope, operations manager for Industrial Products, 2003** —

"Happy, motivated employees equal success." — **Bill Greehey, CEO and chairman of the board for Valero Energy Corp., 2003** —

"You should never stop garnering every bit of wisdom and understanding you can from your life." — **Mike Carter, operations manager for Allied Energy in Birmingham, Ala., 2002** —

"If you can imagine a future and believe in it, there is a natural tendency to get there." — **Mike Batchelor, president and general manager, Aluma Systems USA, 2002** —

154

"One of the most important things is to learn how to convey your thoughts and ideas to other people. You have to be able to communicate, to motivate your workers, to instill your corporate values and to ensure that everyone within the company remains safe on the job." — **R. Dewon Rankin, president of HRI, Inc., 2002** —

"If someone who was just starting out asked me for advice, I would tell them to work hard and do what's right, and you will succeed." — **R.E. "Bob" Parker, president of Repcon, Inc., 2002** —

"If someone were to ask me for my advice, I would tell them to plan, plan, plan. Planning involves setting goals and determining how to reach them. When choices have to be made, it is much easier to make them if a plan is in place to guide your decisions." — **Roby Shields of Louisiana Vegetation Management, 2002** —

"Always keep your eyes open, fill your niche, and don't drift too far away from your specialty." — **Don Breaux of Louisiana Vegetation Management, 2002** —

"To have a solid, successful business takes people qualified in a number of fields. You can't do it alone, so you must hook up with good people. And, you can't be afraid to hire people who know more than you. Once you have developed a core capability, you need to guide the team, but let them do their jobs." — **Gene Silverman, founder and chief technical officer of InTANK Services, Inc., 2002** —

"You have to do a lot of soul searching before you jump into a business. A lot of people think it's easy, but it's not. It's all about having the ability to look at the marketplace and find the best people to work with you." — **John E. Sisson, president and CEO of Quality Inspection Services, Inc., 2002** —

"When you establish yourself as someone who can be counted on, that will carry throughout your career. You must establish a good reputation at the outset." — **Bill Lawson, general manager** of Celanese PBI, 2002 —

"There is no substitute for good customer service, period. Care about the customer and mean it!" — **Jesse Sanders, regional manager for Governor Control Systems, Inc., 2002** —

"Listen to what customers have to say, what is important to them, what makes their job easy, what has or has not worked in the past. Address concerns and ask all the questions necessary to satisfy any application issues." — **Paul Lehman, district manager, southwest region, for Gorman-Rupp, 2002** —

"Give the customer what they require when they require it, but never compromise basic business sense. A business remains a business because it makes a profit." — **Neville J. Barber, president of Expansion Joint Systems, Inc., 2002** —

"Leading a company is similar to being a captain. A ship is essentially a small business. You have to lead by example. You have to encourage people and provide an atmosphere where people can and want to do their very best." — **John Swann, founder, CEO and chief technical officer of Brookdale International Systems, 2002** —

"If you have quality products and excellent service, then the phone will keep ringing." — **Chuck Long, owner of Southern Comfort Shelters, 2001** —

"I have learned that everything takes longer than you think it will and that if you are working smart and hard, stay honest to your core principles, even when it costs you major money, you will succeed in the end. No one succeeds alone. You must have good business relationships, take time to help others win at their business and have a great team." — **Sean Guerre, president and CEO of The TradeFair Group, 2001** —

"If you feel passionately about what you're doing, you'll put everything into it. If I've done anything right in my career, it's that

I've chosen to work for companies with potential growth. After all, it's up to you to apply your own energy. If you don't have passion for the business you're in, you're in the wrong environment. Life is too short to not spend your time doing what you really enjoy." — **Wayland Hicks, chief operating officer of United Rentals, 2001 —**

"Anyone going into business needs to have experience in that particular field. Research your area for a few years before you make any decisions." — **Merlin Hoiseth, chairman of the board of Reactor Services International, 2001 —**

"I have learned more from people doing the work than I could ever have hoped to gain by reading a report. Firsthand experience means everything. I am a strong believer in management by walking around." — **Tony Pritzker, president and CEO of Baker Tanks, Inc., 2001 —**

"By listening to your customers, you're able to focus on making them successful. You can help them meet their goals and objectives. It's a win-win situation." — **Bill Dudley, president of Bechtel Corp.'s Petroleum and Chemical Business Unit, 2001 —**

"Take advantage of all information available. Be curious, join organizations that really know their business and continue to learn. If you improve yourself, you're a more valuable commodity. When you stop learning, that's when life ends." — **John Greco, general manager of Parker Hannifin's Parflex Business Unit, 2001 —**

"My advice to someone considering forming their own company is to really perform a deep personal inventory of why he thinks it makes sense for him to do it, and secondly be honest about whether or not he has the stomach for it." — **Bob Andrews, president and fire chief of Industrial Emergency Services, LLC, 2001 —**

"Growing up, I had two exemplary men as role models. I looked up to both my father and my grandfather, and they taught me that everyone is worthy of being treated with dignity and respect.

They also helped me to realize early in life the importance of family." — **Claude Barber, owner and president of Plant Machine Works, 2001** —

"Be patient and be prepared for slow growth, rather than overnight success. That is the best way to grow a business, and it will be a solid business for a long period of time." — **Charles Ronie, president of STANG Industrial Products, 2001** —

"I don't believe in management, I believe in leadership. I believe that it is possible to influence people that you work with by setting an example and providing guidance or coaching rather than issuing orders and expecting detailed reports. It is important to provide people with a sense of the company's mission and its set of values. From that point, give them the freedom and resources to do what they need in order to accomplish that goal or mission." — **Bill Taylor, president of Delta Processing Equipment, Delta Pump & Power and Delta Technical Services, 2001** —

"It's extremely important to let people know how important they are. Your success depends on them. If there's one thing I've learned, it is that the ability to get along with people is far and away the most important thing in your career." — **Pat DeBusk, vice president of HydroChem Industrial Services, 2001** —

"When people know that you trust them and expect the best from them, they will deliver." — **Dan Robinson, president and CEO of Placid Refining Co., 2000** —

"There have been times when I felt frustrated figuring out a way to do something, and my father [John Paz, owner of Paz Brothers Inc. construction company] gave me inspiration and direction. As he used to tell me, if a man built it, a man can fix it; if a man can imagine it, a man can make it happen." — **John Michael Paz, president and CEO of Godwin Pumps of America, 2000** —

"People have an amazing capacity to be understanding if you're honest and straightforward with them. If something goes wrong, tell them what happened, why it has happened, and how you will solve the problem, and people will work with you." — **Janice Pellar, president of EMCO, 2000** —

"One of the most important things someone just starting out in any business can do is try to be a part of the solution, not the problem. Company owners are always looking for those rare people. If you can go to your boss with a solution, he will be more likely to come to you the next time there is a problem. In the long run, this will lead to more respect, responsibility and money for you. If you do your best, help your boss and provide solutions, the money will follow." — **Len Freemyer, president and CEO of Freemyer Industrial Pressure, 2000** —

"Companies can't be successful if they put customer service anywhere but number one." — **R. Gerald Bennett, president and CEO of Total Safety, 2000** —

"A successful enterprise takes hard work and a very simple philosophy — if you don't take care of your customers, someone else will." — **Mike McKinney, president of LBC PetroUnited, 1999** —

"Never tell people how to do things. Tell them what you want done, and they will surprise you with their ingenuity." — **Craig Anderson, business unit manager for Parker Polyflex, quoting legendary World War II U.S. Army Gen. George S. Patton, 1999** —

"Establishing appropriate goals, developing a realistic plan to achieve those goals, and then realizing the satisfaction of successfully reaching those goals is exhilarating for everyone involved. It fosters pride and excellence in all aspects of work and becomes a self-fulfilling prophecy." — **Phil Hawk, chairman and CEO of Team Industrial Services, 1999** —

"You can buy the best equipment, but if you don't have proper training, your money is wasted." — **Clint Honeycutt, president** and owner of Safety Connection, 1999 —

"Have faith in yourself, have a purpose that you believe in, believe that everything happens for a reason, learn what you can from others, find the right people, and then learn when to get out of the way." — **Mark Conrad, vice president of national sales and marketing for Aggreko, 1999** —

"The best advice I can give to anyone is to do something you truly believe in with people you believe in. And always be true to yourself." — **Carroll Suggs, chairman and CEO of Petroleum Helicopters, Inc., 1999** —

"Never compromise your ethics. Money can be a great motivator, but I strive to balance the requirement for generating a profit with the need to reinvest in business itself. It's not just about making money." — **Darwin H. Simpson, president of Pakhoed Logistics Americas, 1999** —

"Each morning, I take time to consider what I have accomplished so far in meeting the long term goals. I want to know that we're moving in the right direction. There are always little fires to put out, but it's imperative to keep a handle on the future." — **Tony Bessette, vice president of SPIR STAR, Inc., 1999** —

"A lot of people say you need to work smarter, not harder. But, most people who own businesses will agree you have to work longer, harder and smarter if you're going to be successful." — **Alan Van Velkinburgh, president, Houston 2-Way Radio, 1999** —

"Whatever you choose to be a part of, you have to have a strong commitment to what you are doing and a positive attitude. This philosophy, regardless of circumstance, will always enhance your performance." — **Teddy Mansfield, president of Mansfield Industrial Coatings, Inc., 1999** —

"My philosophy is to be honest with those who work for you and those whom you work for. If you let people know what's going on, they're more loyal." — **Richard L. Southers, vice president of operations for Walzel Services, 1999 —**

"When you're honest, people trust you with their concerns. Trust is the key in providing quality work and superior customer service." — **Alton Arnett, product manager for Petris Technology, Terra Air product line, 1999 —**

"I've heard that 60 to 70 percent of new businesses fail. The reason is probably that the owners give up too quickly. Bailing out when things get tough is not an option if you truly want to succeed." — **Mike Windsor, president and CEO of MCS Technologies, 1998 —**

"If you want to start your own business and make a success of it, you will have to work hard. You must set goals and work toward them. Never let anyone deter you from those goals. You will undoubtedly meet more people who say you can't rather than you can. I have been fortunate in having a number of people who looked for the positive and helped my company grow." — **Robert Smith, president and CEO of EarthNet, 1998 —**

"If you're not going forward, then you're going backward. You have to continuously think of ways to better serve your clients and yourself." — **Dan Persha, vice president of Insurance Concepts, 1998 —**

"The best advice I can offer anyone, whatever they're interested in pursuing, is to get all the facts together — all possible information. Then have very strong, well-trained people working for them. Ask for advice from those people and listen to what they have to offer." — **Sherril Baker, CEO of Protherm, Inc., 1998 —**

"Work for your employer like you'll stay forever, but develop yourself as though you'll get laid off tomorrow and have to compete for a new job. Be future oriented and flexible." — **Dr. Gordon Boutwell, president of Soil Testing Engineers, 1998 —**

"If what you are doing is not fun, then you should make it so, or find some other profession that is fun." — **Don Hansen, president of Piping Analysis, Inc., 1998** —

"Through my experiences, I've learned that people skills are number one in doing business. As a manager, keeping your people focused and challenged is paramount, but most important is to give the best satisfaction possible to the customer." — **Tom Comstock, president and chief operating officer of Total Safety, 1998** —

"The key to success or failure is personnel. In most successful organizations, there is one individual who is the driving force behind the company. I try to hire people who are good at what they do and let them operate autonomously to make the company a success." — **Sonny Anderson, founder of Anco and Basic Industries, 1985** —

What Others Have to Say About The BIC Alliance

"We have been a BIC Alliance member since 1996, and each year we've been a front cover sponsor for the June/July issue. We've had good response from our campaigns, and *BIC* has been a great help in delivering our message to the right people." — **Debra Robinson, marketing representative for PBI Performance Products** —

"The *BIC* newsmagazine is very informative. I use it as a source for contractors, new ideas and business information. I also enjoy reading the commentaries from the site managers and industry leaders." — **George Wang, engineering manager of Rhodia Eco Services** —

"*BIC* is proof of what can happen when you combine a good man, Earl Heard, with a good idea. *BIC* has set new standards in publication for industry periodicals." — **Dan Borné, president of the Louisiana Chemical Association** —

"We have received tangible results — an initiative with an $8 million-a-year revenue potential — as a result of the [first front cover] campaign. The first insertion of our BIC campaign generated that lead." — **Scott Thibodeaux, vice president of business development for Atlantic Scaffolding Co.** —

"Don't let procrastination set in — make a commitment to using *BIC* in every way you can. Even if you use just 80 percent of what they have to offer, you will see results." — **Bill Brossart, corporate director of marketing for The Brock Group** —

"I would like to thank the folks at *BIC* for their excellent assistance in getting prospective buyers and I together for the purpose of selling our surplus environmental equipment. We are pleased with their prompt service and professionalism." — **Bill DeLang, site assessment & remediation, Chevron Products Co.** —

"Since starting our campaign with *BIC*, we have seen an increase in our work throughout industry. I have received positive feedback about our ads from people in industry who read *BIC*. We think *BIC* is a very effective way to get the good news about our company out to our primary target audience." — **Eddie Garza, president of Turnaround Welding Services** —

"We have used *BIC* for everything from business referrals to fact finding for the industry. It was *BIC* that first approached us on behalf of CEI for the purchase of our transportation division. There is a definite benefit to bringing in a third-party negotiator. They can help each participant remove the emotion from the deal. They are able to focus on critical issues in getting the deal accomplished." — **Rick Conway, former CEO of Gulf South Systems** —

"If you're in the industry and want to succeed, it's a great idea to become a BIC Alliance member. It's only going to hurt you to not advertise in *BIC*. Whether it's the cherrypicking of the database, taking advantage of mailing directly to your individual clients or getting the responses, you definitely get your money's worth with a *BIC* campaign." — **George More, president of Mascoat Products** —

"Our experience with *The Leisure Connection (TLC)* has had many benefits. In addition to the ad space we've paid for, *TLC* has done feature articles on Joshua Creek Ranch, printed photos of the ranch and even come here to experience firsthand the spectacular wingshooting, dining and accommodations enjoyed by our many guests. It's been beneficial as well as pleasant doing business with the folks at the BIC Alliance." — **Ann Kercheville, president of Joshua Creek Ranch** —

"Our area of specialty is destination marketing, i.e. golf course communities and upscale real estate. We've placed several of our clients in *TLC* because of its unique audience. We've found that *TLC* is the best place to reach mid- to upper-level management in the Gulf South." — **Jack Kerigan, president and CEO of Kerigan Marketing** —

"*TLC* has assisted us in marketing the Bay Area Houston region as a weekend and vacation destination by publicizing our region's attractions, special events and activities to our targeted audience along the Gulf Coast. We value our relationship with *TLC* and its staff, who have consistently assisted us in offering affordable cooperative marketing opportunities for our industry partners throughout the region." — **Pam Summers, executive director of the Bay Area Houston Convention and Visitors Bureau** —

"From running just one ad and article in BIC, we had success. We found a couple of new customers as a direct result of BIC." — **Steve Earney, vice president of D.L. Ricci** —

"We take advantage of every opportunity to grow our company. BIC offers many marketing avenues — extras that come without cost — that support our growth goals. We feel that Oilind's professionalism has been recognized because of these opportunities." — **Kirk Peda, president of Oilind Safety** —

"Earl is very interactive with the attendees and his seminar applies to everyone. The various sales techniques he taught us were things I had never heard of, but they were techniques that I can begin to apply." — **Jamie Reesby, attendance development coordinator for The TradeFair Group** —

"Earl's seminar was absolutely beneficial to our company. His seminar is realistic, and our salespeople really enjoyed it. The information is practical, and his sales techniques are proven." — **Paul Tyree, sales manager for the industrial division of WSI Total Safety, a division of Total Safety US Inc.** —

BIC Alliance Members
2004-2005

Listed below are the BIC and TLC partners whose patronage helped make the publication of this book possible. Please remember to use their products and/or services for whatever needs you may have, whether they be related to business, industry or leisure.

-ACS Industries
-Adler Tank Rentals
-AEC Design Group
-Aerotek/Ethicom Associates
-Alloy Products
-AlphaGraphics
-AltairStrickland
-Aluma Enterprises
-American Society of
 Nondestructive Testing
-Ameritek
-Anchor Lamina
-Antientropics
-Apex Engineering Products
-ASME
-Atlantic Scaffolding
-AWC II, Inc.
-Aztec Tent Services
-Baker Industrial Concrete
-Baker Printing
-Baker Tanks
-Barnhart Crane & Rigging Co.
-BaseLine Data
-Baton Rouge Press

-Bay Area Industrial Contractors
-Bird Tec
-Blue Flash Express
-BOLTTECH
-Boutin's Restaurant
-The Brock Group
-Bronco Construction
-Buckeye Gulf Coast Pipelines
-BW Technologies
-Calgon Carbon
-Carhartt, Inc.
-Cat Tech, Inc.
-Catalyst Services
-CEDA, Inc.
-Centrifuges Unlimited
-Certified Safety Specialists
-CFM/VR-TESCO
-Chillco, Inc.
-Classified USA
-Cleveland Wrecking Co.
-Clock Spring Co.
-Coating Services
-Columbia Scaffolding Services
-CONAM Inspection

-CONEXPO-CON/AGG
-Continuum Chemical Corp.
-Cooperheat-MQS
-Covers Unlimited
-Crown Enterprises
-Danos & Curole
-DeBusk Industrial Services
-Deepwater Corrosion Services
-DeHumidification Technologies
-DeLane's Ad Specialties
-Delta Tech Service
-DeltaValve
-Diamond Refractory Services
-DISA, Inc.
-Diversified Business
 Communications
-D.L. Ricci Corp.
-Drury Hotels
-Duratherm, Inc.
-Eagle Construction &
 Environmental Services
-Eagle Industries
-EMCO Technologies
-Emergency Response Training
-Emission Monitoring Service, Inc.
 (EMSI)
-Empire Scaffold
-Environmental Containment
 Systems
-EPSCO International
-Evergreen Environmental Services
-Expansion Joint Systems
-Expansion Seal Technology Group
-FabEnCo, Inc.

-The Farm Golf Club
-The File Depot
-First Advantage Corp.
-Fishbone Solutions
-Flexitallic
-Flow International Corp.
-Flow Logic International
-Flowserve Corp.
-Furmanite Worldwide
-Galco
-Gardner Denver Water
 Jetting Systems
-Geotek Industrial Distributors
-Glove Guard
-GLY-TECH Service
-Godwin Pumps of America
-Golf Cars of Houston
-Gorman-Rupp
-GOTAR
-Grainger Supply
-Greater New Orleans Hotels
-Greystone Castle Sporting Club
-H2A Environmental
-Hampton Inn & Suites
 Houston Medical Center
-Henderson Auctions
-Hertz Equipment Rental
-High Pressure Equipment Co.
-Hilton Houston Hobby Airport
-HMHTTC Response, Inc.
-Hodges Corporate Holdings
-Holiday Inn Select-
 Baton Rouge, La.
-Houston Area Safety Council

-HRI, Inc.
-Hyatt Regency New Orleans
-Hydro Tank, Inc.
-Hydrochem Industrial Services
-Independent Liquid Terminals
 Association
-InduMar Products
-Industrial Cooling Tower Services
-Industrial Performance Services
-Industrial Safety & Health, Inc.
 (ISH)
-Industrial Safety Training Council
-Industrial Surfacing Corp.
-Infinity Maintenance
-Infinity Trading Co.
-Innovative EHS
-Inter Plan Systems
-ISO Panels
-Jet Edge
-J.F. Ahern Co.
-Joshua Creek Ranch
-Jotun Paints
-JV Industrial Companies
-K2 Industrial Services
-KeepSafe
-Knight Industrial Services
-Layher, Inc.
-LHR Services & Equipment
-LOBOS
-Louisiana Chemical Pipe, Valve
 & Fitting
-Louisiana Dept. of Economic
 Development
-Louisiana Dept. of Environmental
 Quality

-Louisiana Dept. of Labor
-Louisiana-Mississippi Carpenters
 Regional Council
-Louisiana Rents
-Mach Industrial Group
-Marketects, Inc.
-Mary Kay O'Connor Process
 Safety Center
-Mascoat Products
-MB Industries
-MCCI
-Mechanical Integrity
-Medical Plaza Mobile
 Surveillance
-Merichem Chemicals & Refinery
 Services
-Meridian Equipment
-Merrick Impact Systems
-M, G & B Services
-MHT Access Services
-Mikron Infrared
-Milling Benson Woodward
-Mississippi State University
-Modern Group
-Moran Printing
-MSA
-National Center for Construction
 Education & Research
-National Drum Disposal
-National Institute for Storage Tank
 Management
-Neco Trucking
-NEO Safety Foundation
-Neptune Research
-New Century Fabricators

-New Orleans Metropolitan
 Convention & Visitors Bureau
-Nimlok-Lafayette
-NLB Corp.
-NPRA
-Office Automation
-Offshore Technology Conference
-Oilind Safety
-Onsite Water Corp. (Waterboy)
-Onyx Environmental Services
-PacTec
-Panametrics-NDT
-Pappas Restaurants
-ParkerHannifin
-PBI Performance Products
-Pennwell Publishing
-Petrochemical Services
-PetroSafe Technologies
-PI Integrated Systems
-Plant Performance Services (P2S)
-P-M-E Equip
-Port of Greater Baton Rouge, La.
-Praxair Services
-Prime Information
-Process Strainers, Inc.
-Protherm Services Group
-Providence Engineering
 & Environmental
-PS Doors
-PS Land and Marine
-Quality Inspection Services
-RAE Systems
-Rain for Rent
-Reactor Services International
-Refined Technologies

-Remote Access Technology
-Rental Service Corp.
-Repcon
-Rhino Linings
-Rio Grande Rancho
-RKI Instruments
-Robert J. Jenkins & Co.
-Roco Rescue
-Safety Council
-SafetyTools
-Safway Services
-Scaffolding Dynamics
-SCAFFTAG///SAFETRAK
-Separation Systems Consultants,
 Inc. (SSCI)
-SET, Inc.
-Shaw Maintenance
-Shell Landing
-Sheraton Inner Harbour
-SI Group
-Sipco Surface Protection
-Society for Protective Coatings
-SOLA Communications
-South Shore Harbour Resort
-Southern Comfort Shelters
-Southland Fire & Safety
 Equipment
-Southwest Insulation Contractors
 Association
-SPIR STAR
-Steel Associates
-Strategic Asset Management
-Structural Group
-Success Images
-Sulzer Chemtech USA

169

-Summit Training Source
-Superior Energies
-Superior Plant Services
-Tank Consultants, Inc.
-TankCo Services/Vapor
 Combustion Technologies
-TD Williamson
-Team Industrial Services
-TEEX-Emergency
 Services Training Institute
-Terra Environmental Technologies
-Texas Chemical Council
-Texas Commission on
 Environmental Quality
-Texas Industrial Specialties
-Texas Molecular
-Texas ReExcavation
-Third Coast Engineering Corp.
-Thomas J. Lipscomb, Ph.D.
-Thorpe Corp.
-TIGG Corp.
-TorcUP, Inc.
-Total Industrial Services
-Total Safety/WSI
-The TradeFair Group
-TriStar PetroServ
-Triton Industries
-TTS Performance Systems/CPPM
-Tulane University EMBA Program
-Turbomachinery Laboratory
-Turnaround Management
 Company
-Turnaround Welding Services
-Turner Industries
-UHP Projects

-United Access
-United Services
-Universal Plant Services
-University of Nevada Fire
 Safety Academy
-U.S. Oil Recovery
-Vopak Industrial Services
-Vulcan Finned Tubes
-Water Environment
 Federation/WEFTEC
-Water Jet Technology Association
-Weatherford Gemoco
-Web Devices
-Webco Industries
-West Baton Rouge Tourist
 Information and Conference
 Center
-Wolf Creek Co.
-Worksafe
-Wyatt Field Service
-Wyndham New Orleans Hotel
 at Canal Place
-XServ, Inc.

170

The Leisure Connection Members
2004-2005

-777 Ranch
-Advanced Office Systems
-Alaska's Boardwalk Lodge
-Alaska River Guides
-Aqua Terra Storage Plus
-Arco Distributors, Inc.
-Ascension Marine
-Ascension Properties
-At the Helm
-Austin Convention & Visitors
 Bureau
-Baker Printing
-Barge Inn
-Baton Rouge, La., Pro Bass
 Challenge
-Bay Area Houston Convention &
Visitors Bureau
-Bay Area Sailing School
-The Beach Club Gulf Shores, Ala.
-Beaumont, Texas, Convention &
Visitors Bureau
-Becuna Charters
-Big Lake Guide Service
-Billeann's Flowers & Gifts
-Boogie Bus
-Boutin's Restaurant
-Brady's Landing
-Brazosport, Texas, Convention &
Visitors Council
-Broussard's Restaurant

-Calloway Inn & Suites
-Canyon of the Eagles
-Capital City Grill
-Capt. Elliott's Party Boats
-Captain John L.'s Charters
-Carlson Wagonlit Travel
-Carter Plantation
-Chamberlain-Hunt Academy
-City of Bandera, Texas
-City of Boerne, Texas
-City of Nassau Bay, Texas
-City of Seabrook, Texas
-City of Webster, Texas
-Claudio's Ristorante
-Clear Lake Charter Boats
-Coast2Coast Printing
 & Promotions
-Constellation Pointe
-Cotton Mesa Trophy Elk
-Courtyard by Marriott at
 Craft Farms
-CruiseOne/Carnival Cruise Lines
-Cypress Bend Golf Resort
-Dallas Safari Club
-DeAngelo's Pizzeria Co.
-Del Lago Golf Resort
 & Conference Center
-DeLane's Ad Specialties
-Delfin Diving
-Destination League City, Texas

-Diamond Guide Service
-Diamond "W" Ranch
-Don Sanders Insurance
-Douglas, Inc.
-Down Home Adventures
-Drury Hotels
-Eagle Pointe Golf Club
 & Recreation Complex
-El Canelo Ranch
-Exotics Plus
-Family RV Center
-The Farm Golf Club
-Flying L Guest Ranch
-Ford Park
-Dr. Thomas Foster, D.D.S.
-Galveston Island Convention
 & Visitors Bureau
-Gaylord Texan
-Golden Ranch Plantation
-Gran Chaco Adventures
-Greater New Orleans Hotels
-Greystone Castle Sporting Club
-Gulf Coast Yacht Group
-Gulf County, Florida
-Hacienda Don Quixote
-Hampton Inn & Suites Houston
Medical Center
-Heartland Wildlife Ranches
-H&H Outfitters
-Hilton Houston Hobby Airport
-Hodges Corporate Holdings
-Holiday Inn Chateau Lemoyne
-Holiday Inn French Quarter
-Holiday Inn NASA, Houston
-Houma, La., Area Convention &

Visitors Bureau
-Houston Safari Club
-Hunan Chinese Restaurant
-Hyatt Regency New Orleans
-Inn of the Hills
-Innovative RV
-The Island Golf Club
-J/B Adventures & Safaris
-Jo Ann Stockwill
-Jones Creek Café & Oyster Bar
-Joshua Creek Ranch
-Keels & Wheels Concours
 d'Elegance
-Keepsafe
-Keller Williams Real Estate/
Toni House
-Kerrville, Texas, Convention &
Visitors Bureau
-Kicker Fish Bait Co.
-Lafayette, La., Convention
 & Visitors Commission
-LaQuinta Inn and
 Suites Seabrook, Texas
-Las Brisas Beach House
-Livingston Parish Convention
 & Visitors Bureau
-Lodge of Louisiana
-Lone Star Flight Museum
-Louisiana Aircraft
-Louisiana Hunting Adventures
-Louisiana Office of Culture,
 Recreation & Tourism
-LSU Fire & Emergency Training
 Institute
-Lunden Limousine Service

-Majestic Hunting Tours
-Majestic Ventures
-Malcolm Travel
-Mardi Gras Productions
-Marker 1 Marina
-McLavy Ltd.
-MCM Eleganté Hotel
-Medicine Bow Lodge
-Medina River Ranch
-Menger Hotel
-Michael R. Choate & Co., CPAs
-Michaul's on St. Charles
-Moody Gardens
-Moran Printing
-National Whitetail Association
-NEO Safety Foundation
-New Braunfels, Texas, Convention
& Visitors Bureau
-New Orleans Hornets
-New Orleans Metropolitan
Convention & Visitors Bureau
-Orion Outfitters
-Palo Alto Plantation
-Pappas Restaurants
-ParadiseCruise.com
-Parker Guide Service
-Pheasant Meadows Outfitters
-Pure Concepts
-Radisson Hill Country Resort &
Spa, San Antonio
-Radisson Hotel & Suites, Austin
-Red Devil Charters
-Red River Bar-B-Que
-RE/MAX by the Bay
-Rio Grande Rancho

-Rough Creek Lodge
-Royal Sonesta
-San Antonio Convention
& Visitors Bureau
-Schlitterbahn
-Seawillow Sailing
-SeaWorld Adventure Park,
San Antonio
-Shell Landing
-Shonto Ranch
-Six Flags New Orleans
-Soulful Images
-South Shore Harbour
Country Club
-South Shore Harbour Resort
& Conference Center
-Southeast Louisiana Convention
& Visitors Bureau
-Success Images
-Tapatio Springs Resort &
Conference Center
-T Bar M Ranch
-Texas Renaissance Festival
-Thibodeaux's Restaurant
-Thomas J. Lipscomb, Ph.D.
-Timber Creek Golf Club
-Treads & Care Tire Co.
-Trophy King Lodge
-The Waterfront
-West Baton Rouge Tourist
Information & Conference Center
-What's Cookin'
-White Antler Ranch
-Wildlife Systems, Inc.
-Wings Over Houston

173

-WurstFest

-Wyndham Anatole

-Wyndham New Orleans Hotel
 at Canal Place

-Y O Ranch Resort & Hotel

A Word About BIC Publishing

In 2004, during a speaking engagement at Chamberlain-Hunt Academy in Port Gibson, Miss., where my daughter Dane graduated from high school, I was amazed at the number of young folks today who are interested in careers in entrepreneurship, management and sales. It's also intrigued me to learn that entrepreneurship is alive and well in America — there are more than 17 million entrepreneurs in the nation alone. Also, during a visit to the 2005 New Orleans Writers Conference, I was excited to discover that one of the fastest growing segments in publishing is faith and spirituality.

Since early childhood, I've been an avid reader, and I particularly enjoy books about how different people have overcome various forms of adversity. I also subscribe to more than 100 publications that are either work- or leisure-related in order to learn and search for creative marketing ideas, topics to explore, etc. Many of the articles I write in BIC are inspired by the sermons of ministers and priests I've met and whose television programs I've watched over the years, and by motivational speakers. They're also inspired by the many executives and entrepreneurs we've interviewed over the years.

One of my goals is to publish books and offer training and speaker services that inspire our youth to consider careers in entrepreneurship, management and sales. I am shown here speaking to youths at Chamberlain-Hunt Academy in Port Gibson, Miss., about overcoming adversity and entrepreneurship.

Everywhere I go I ask folks of all ages what types of articles and books they like to read. Our research indicates growing

175

interest and growth opportunities not only for entrepreneurship and faith but also the publishing of memoirs, company histories and autobiographies.

We've learned that as baby boomers grow older and retire, they're more interested not only in the pursuit of leisure but also for inner peace and helping make the world a better place. This tells me that wholesome reading and writing is alive and well and knows no age limit. (It almost brought tears to my eyes recently when I walked into the bedroom of my granddaughters Hannah, 10, and Mary, 7, to find them enjoying the adventure of reading in their free time.)

Among our possible future projects are an expanded Alligator Management & Marketing and Sales Training manual, a book about the expanding role of faith in industry, and, perhaps, a book about youths and entrepreneurship. Reading back over the past 25 years of *The Training Coordinator* and the *BIC* newsmagazine is like reading a history book about the energy business. We've written so many wonderful feature articles and interviewed so many successful executives and entrepreneurs that it hardly seems fair to mention some of them and not all. The markets for books on entrepreneurship and faith seem endless, as we've seen just by talking to industry folks from organizations such as API, NPRA, the Texas Chemical Council, the Louisiana Chemical Association, Associated Builders and Contractors, and the Oilfield

We at the BIC Alliance plan to partner with business, industry and community leaders such as East Baton Rouge Parish Mayor-President Kip Holden to help inspire people from all walks of life to shoot for success by sharing with them our story of faith, hard work and perseverance.

Christian Fellowship.

We plan to explore the world of self-publishing because, as one author explained, selling a book to a publishing house is as difficult today as turning a cruise ship around. And as a famed journalist and novelist said at the 2005 New Orleans Writers Conference, every person has a story waiting to be told. Twenty-five thousand people in America consider themselves writers, and there are more than 175,000 books written each year. We've met several hundred aspiring authors who began as journalists, librarians, school teachers, and even petroleum engineers and scientists.

It's been estimated that only one book in every 50,000 published will be a bestseller. With this book, I don't aspire to write a bestseller, but I do intend to tell an inspiring story that others can relate to and utilize in their everyday lives.

If you feel that your story is interesting and/or inspiring and would like to share it with others, feel free to contact us at (800) 460-4242 to learn more about our custom publishing service.

If you'd like to order additional copies of this book, you can do so online at www.bicpublishing.com.*

---

* In July 2005, as we neared completion of It's What We Do Together That Counts, we launched a new Web site — www.bicpublishing.com. On this new Web site, you can learn more about each of our publications and read excerpts from and reviews of this book. You can also learn about our custom publishing service, our Alligator Management & Marketing seminars and our turnkey event planning service.

We expect to use this site not only to provide information on our publishing, management consulting and training services, but also to create a "BIC Bookstore," where we will offer books from other publishers about entrepreneurship, faith, overcoming adversity, management, marketing and sales, in addition to books published by our company.

Suggested Readings

— The Bible: New International Version

— *Anatomy of an Entrepreneur: The Story of Joseph Jacobs, Founder of Jacobs Engineering*, by Joseph J. Jacobs

— *Nuts!: Southwest Airlines' Crazy Recipe for Business and Personal Success*, by Kevin Freiberg and Jackie Freiberg

— *Split Second Choice: The Power of Attitude*, by Jim Winner

— *Your Best Life Now*, by Joel Osteen

— *Who Moved My Cheese?*, by Spencer Johnson, M.D.

— *Walt Disney: An American Original*, by Bob Thomas

— *Winning Every Day*, by Lou Holtz

— *The Prize: The Epic Quest for Oil, Money & Power*, by Daniel Yergin

— *You Are My Sunshine: The Jimmie Davis Story*, by Gus Weill

— *Minute Motivators for Leaders*, by Stan Tolar

— *The 22 Immutable Laws of Marketing,* by Al Ries and Jack Trout

— *Guerrilla Marketing*, by Jay Conrad Levinson

— *The Happy Road to Success*, by Fred J. Greer Jr.

— *Communicate With Confidence*, by Dianna Booker

— *How to Become CEO: The Rules for Rising to the Top of Any Organization*, by Jeffrey J. Fox

— *The Millionaire Next Door,* by Dr. Thomas Stanley and Dr. William Danko

— *Confessions of a Management Consultant Turned CEO*, by Anita Simonton

— *Nonverbal Communications in Human Interaction*, by Mark Knopp

— *The 100 Simple Secrets of Happy People*, by David Niven, Ph.D.

— *Developing Tomorrow's Manager Today*, by Francis Dinsmore

— *Managing Growth: Keys to Success for Expanding Companies*, by Gay Weismantel and Walter Kesling Jr.

— *Onassis: Aristotle and Christina*, by L. J. Davis

— *Trump: The Art of the Deal*, by Tony Schwartz

— *Iacocca: An Autobiography*, by Lee Iacocca with William Novak

— *Memory: How It Works & How to Improve It*, by Roy Gallant

— *Flight of the Buffalo*, by James Belesseo and Ralph Stayer

— *God's Psychiatry: But God Can*, by Chabo Allen and Robert Ozmont

— *Chicken Soup for the Soul*, by Jack Canfield and Mark Victor Hansen

— *Best Speeches by Eminent Speakers*, by Grenville Kleiser

— *The Path: Creating Your Mission Statement for Work and Life*, by Laurie Jones

— *No Ordinary Time: Franklin & Eleanor Roosevelt, The Home Front in WWII*, by Doris Goodwin

— *The Courage to be Rich*, by Suze Orman

— *It Only Takes Everything You've Got*, by Julio Melara

— *In Search of Excellence*, by Tom Peters and Robert Waterman Jr.

— *Powerful Writing*, by Richard Anderson

— *How to Think Like a CEO*, by D.A. Brown

— *Leadership 101*, by John Maxwell

— *Secrets of Closing Sales*, by Charles Roth and Roy Alexander

— *Selling 101*, by Michael McGaellery

— *Soft Selling in a Hard World*, by Jerry Voss

— *You Don't Say*, by Vernon Prizer

— *AMA Complete Guide to Small Business Marketing*, by Kenneth J. Cook

— *Phillips and Duncan's Marketing Principles and Methods*, by James M. Carman and Kenneth P. Uhl

— *Marketing Masters*, by Gene Walden and Edmund Lawler

— *Dare to Lead: Proven Principles of Effective Leadership*, by Byrd Baggett

— *Entrepreneur Magazine's 303 Marketing Tips*, by Rieva Lesonsky and Leann Anderson

— *Mindgames: Phil Jackson's Long Strange Journey*, by Roland Lazenby

— *How to Close Every Sale*, by Joe Girard with Robert L. Shook

— *The Marketing Plan: How to Prepare and Implement It*, by William M. Luther

— *Secrets of the World's Top Sales Performers*, by Christine Harvey

— *Direct Marketing Rules of Thumb*, by Nat G. Bodian

— *Underdog Marketing: Successful Strategies for Outmarketing the Leader*, by Edmund Lawler

179

— *Ed McMahon's Superselling: Performance Techniques for High-Volume Sales*, by Ed McMahon with Warren Jamison

— *The Purpose Driven Life*, by Rick Warren

— *Maximizing Misfortune: Turning Life's Failures Into Success*, by Jerome Edmondson

— *Leading With My Chin*, by Jay Leno

— *Prosperity: The Choice is Yours*, by Kenneth Copeland

— *Closing the Leadership Gap: Why Women Can and Must Help Run the World*, by Marie C. Wilson

— *Give Me a Break*, by John Stossel

— *The Exceptional Presenter: A Proven Formula to Open Up! And Own the Room*, by Timothy J. Koegel

— *Success One Day at a Time*, by John C. Maxwell

— *How to Retire Happy, Wild and Free*, by Ernie J. Zelinski

— *The Adventure of Retirement*, by Guild A. Fetridge

— *This Cajun Ain't Bashful*, by Daily Berard

— *Dave's Way*, by Dave Thomas

— *Overcoming Hurt and Anger*, by Dwight L. Carlson, M.D.

— *The Making of a Bestseller*, by Brian Hill and Dee Power

Order Form

If you would like to obtain informaiton to order additional copies
of this book, please fill out the form below:

Sixty-two years in the making, *It's What We Do Together That Counts* is the story of BIC Alliance CEO and Founder Earl Heard's lifelong journey to achieve his dream of becoming a successful entrepreneur. Combining a lifetime of anecdotal wisdom with insight from more than 100 successful executives and entrepreneurs in business and industry, the book is a great guide for anyone seeking greater peace, happiness and success, regardless of age.

Soft Cover: $20 each plus $4 shipping and sales tax where applicable.

Hard Cover: $35 each plus $5 shipping and sales tax where applicable.

Ordering Information:

Type of book: _____ Quantity: _____ Total: _____

Name: _____

Company: _____ **Title:** _____

Address: _____

City/State: _____ **Zip:** _____

Phone (REQUIRED): _____ **Fax:** _____

E-Mail: _____

Web Address: _____

- **Please mail to: P.O. Box 40166, Baton Rouge, LA 70835.**
  Make checks payable to The BIC Alliance.

OR ORDER ONLINE AT WWW.BICPUBLISHING.COM

To book a speaking engagement with Earl Heard and/or an
Alligator Management & Marketing seminar, contact the BIC
Alliance at the address above or online at web address listed or
call (800) 460-4242.

Thank you for your order!

181

"If you want to know what patience, hard work, family, faith and a never-give-up attitude have to do with being a successful entrepreneur, then this book is a must-read."
                    — Jim Culpepper of Greener Trees Louisiana

"This is a great book. Earl Heard is the most optimistic person I've ever known. He is a true winner because of his attitude."
                    — David Starkey, president and CEO of Empire Scaffold

"Earl Heard and the BIC Alliance success story prove once again that the American dream is alive and well."
                    — Michael R. Choate, president of Michael R. Choate & Co., CPAs

"Earl Heard's story is inspirational. He shows us that a love of God and family and very, very hard work can overcome adversity and produce success in life and in business."
— Peter A. Mayer, chairman of the board of Peter A. Mayer Advertising

"Through the years I have ministered to many people who have felt that they had no hope and that life had crumbled around them. Some of those individuals I have sent to Earl Heard so that they could hear his story about blessings through hardship. I am thrilled that now I can give them *It's What They Do Together That Counts* so they can see how hope can come out of tragedy. There are many truths and character-building principles in this book that can generate hope in one's soul and help people see clearly the path to success."
                    — Ron Tyndall, associate pastor of
                    Parkview Baptist Church in Baton Rouge, La.

"When I reference 'Earl Heard' in the dictionary of life it displays a man driven by faith, compassion, family, high moral standards, perseverance, focus, unbounded optimism, dedication to fairness and the willingness to help others succeed. I have been blessed to have worked with him for over 25 years and gained the valuable insight on the art of doing business in an ethical manner and not compromising my principle of treating people like you wish to be treated."

— Kent Wasmuth, area director of sales and marketing for the
Wyndham New Orleans Hotel at Canal Place

"Earl Heard touches us with a simple but powerful message of hardship and success. In a day when our younger generation is overwhelmed with issues and choices, obstacles and negative vibes, it is refreshing to find a cheerleader for the power of encouragement, proper training and service to others."

— Roy Green, general manager of South Shore Harbour Resort

"Earl Heard has faced adversity and has shown us in his book that only perseverance can overcome the hardship that life brings. He is indeed a man of strong faith in God and makes us realize that it takes grit, savvy and a strong belief in oneself to be successful. He also shows that achieving one's dream is possible. *It's What We Do Together That Counts* is a primer for anyone who wants to start their own business. Mr. Heard describes the process in a way that no textbook can."

— J. Ronald Guillory, director of human resources,
Valero New Orleans, LLC

"Earl's story is truly fascinating. It is a story of how lessons learned early in life have turned situations of utter failure into undeniable success. It is an inspiring story of the pursuit of one man's dream, woven with learnings of perseverance, faith and a lot of hard work."

— Thomas Brinsko, president and chief operating officer of the BIC
Alliance and Ind-Viro Search